CRACKING

PHILOSOPHY

YOU, THIS BOOK AND 3,000 YEARS OF THOUGHT

CRACKING
PHILOSOPHY

YOU, THIS BOOK AND 3,000 YEARS OF THOUGHT

DR MARTIN COHEN

CASSELL
ILLUSTRATED

An Hachette UK Company
www.hachette.co.uk

First published in Great Britain in 2016 by Cassell,
a division of
Octopus Publishing Group Ltd
Carmelite House
50 Victoria Embankment
London EC4Y 0DZ
www.octopusbooks.co.uk

ISBN 978-1-84403-806-0

A CIP catalogue record for this book is available from the
British Library.

Printed and bound in China

10 9 8 7 6 5 4 3 2

Editorial Director Trevor Davies
Editor Pauline Bache
Production Controller Sarah-Jayne Johnson

Created for Octopus Publishing by
Tall Tree Ltd
Project Editor Rod Green
Designer Malcolm Parchment

CONTENTS

INTRODUCTION

There is a particular tension in the title of this book which may strike some readers. 'Cracking' is both about 'cracking open' and about breaking, damaging. Are we about to ruin the elegant facade of philosophy, by hitting it with a hammer? Or is the plan more to carefully spin the wheels on it, in the manner of an expert safecracker? At the end, will we end up with a few nuts –or some valuable jewels?

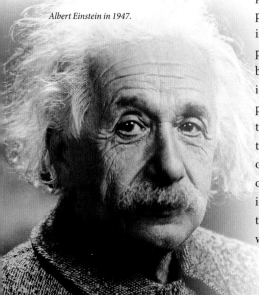

Albert Einstein in 1947.

Of that, be assured the answer is the latter. Nonetheless, in the process we will have to ask some very tough questions and even break a few venerable conventions about what philosophy both 'is' and what philosophy has been over the centuries. Be prepared to abandon your preconceptions! Of course, there are philosophical facts, but if you want an introduction to the great issues of philosophy, which is what this book provides, then you will also end up with plenty of unresolved and perhaps irresolvable problems. There is a general progression in time, as the book unfolds, but it is not a straitjacket. For example, if it seems helpful to compare Zeno's paradoxes of motion to Einstein's theories of relativity, then you will find the discussions sitting alongside each other in the same chapter. The advantage of this approach is that each chapter is independent, but sub-sections within them should make perfect sense even when read in isolation. A possible disadvantage is that the views, for example, of a particular philosopher are not necessarily all grouped together but may be scattered across several chapters (the index reunites such material).

With this in mind, let us now offer a brisk 'Cook's Tour' of the book, which can act as a guide to the overall project. The tour starts, but you by no means have to, at Chapter One on 'Mysteries and Wondering'. This chapter introduces the main themes of the book, starting with the writings of Thales and Parmenides in Ancient Greece, the thinkers whose ideas actually make up much of the substance of the better known writings of Plato. It is Parmenides' 'path of truth' that Plato follows in his bid to transform philosophy via the eternal triad of 'Truth, Beauty, and the Good'. These great concepts inspired his theory of the 'Heavenly Forms' – perhaps philosophy's most mysterious entities, and the ones that for Plato created shape and order out of the flux of the universe.

This first chapter also takes a close look at the Ancient Chinese philosophies

that underlie so much Western thinking. Confucius, Lao Tzu, Mencius and Chuang Tzu offer timeless insights without, of course, agreeing. But then, neither did Aristotle and Plato, and one was supposed to be the pupil of the other.

Chapter Two focuses on to the 'Golden Age' of philosophy and the writings of Plato, one of the primary protagonists of the age, whose words provided the foundations of much future philosophical debate. Yet Plato was by no means an originator. Rather, he was representing the debates of his forebears, and in particular the ideas of Pythagoras. But where did the Pythagoreans get their inspiration? The answer is a lot more internationalized than conventional histories allow. Pythagoras seems to have travelled widely, absorbing many powerful notions from the East and from Egyptian and Persian scholars.

Chapter Three considers the relationship of philosophy and religion. These days the two are often at loggerheads – not so much two sides of the same coin as two angrily opposed factions. Yet this recent hostility hides a greater and more important historical symbiosis. After all, in philosophy, as Gustave Flaubert once put it, 'a small dose of science leads away from religion, a large dose brings us right back to it'.

Western philosophy is often obsessed with death, which is a legacy not so much of the influence of the Christian church, as of a much older mysticism. It is the subtext, too, of the long death scene in Plato's dialogue called *The Apology*, which is supposedly centred on the efforts of Socrates to defend himself against the charges of corrupting the young, in particular into not believing in the gods, or at least not the right ones. Fatalism and predestination remained a key theme for medieval philosophy,

There is another way of looking at philosophical ethics – as the study of evil. In doing so, the specialists here are surely the two saintly scholars, Augustine and Thomas Aquinas. Augustine recorded all his personal failings in insalubrious detail in his surprisingly racy account called *The Confessions*. It is to Augustine

that we owe the dubious concept of 'original sin' – the kind that makes even newborn babies a little bit 'evil'.

Aquinas was a great codifier of the Church, ruling on practical issues and setting out policy positions both on great matters, such as 'when war is justified', to minutiae, such as whether or not the Saints' names were really written on a scroll somewhere in heaven. Historically, though, his main influence is his insistence that arguments should be based, not on documents of faith, but on reasons and statements. This was a major advance and laid the groundwork for the next stage in the story of philosophy, which is the subject matter of Chapters Four through to Six.

This is where philosophy becomes the kind of thing that is today put in encyclopedias under that heading and studied in colleges. It kicks off with Descartes (although he was himself echoing the medieval thinkers) and soon becomes firmly devoted to the dispassionate analysis of arguments and ideas.

From the Renaissance on, philosophy becomes the hand-maiden not only to science but also to society, and society is the focus of Chapter Seven, 'Capitalism, and the Rational Man', which examines the writings of figures like Hegel, Marx and Adam Smith.

Chapter Eight, 'A Fork In The Road', takes a look at the psychological theories of the gloomy German, Schopenhauer, the erratic Rousseau and the witty Kierkegaard.

The German philosopher, Arthur Schopenhauer.

Chapter Nine, 'Language, Truth And Logic', on the other hand, presents a very dry, abstract kind of philosophy, rooted in the study of the workings of language and the belief that it can – and should – be made more 'logical'. Here, Leibniz, Bertrand Russell and Wittgenstein make the running, but it is also the occasion to revisit the work of Aristotle who, after all, wrote the first major work on philosophical logic, as well as to explore some very different recent ideas on the workings of language.

Finally, to Chapter Ten, 'Beyond Science – Philosophers Still Searching For Wisdom' and a look at some of the philosophical debates raging today in the social sciences: from Thomas Kuhn arguing that science proceeds via paradigm shifts to theories about the myriad unexpected ways that words acquire their meanings. And, to close, we look in on the neuroscientific search for answers to the mysteries of 'how we think', an approach that resurrects the 16th-century suspicion that each of us is just a rather complicated machine.

CHAPTER 1
MYSTERIES AND WONDERING: WHERE IT ALL STARTED — THE FIRST PHILOSOPHERS

'We have to remember that what we observe is not nature in itself but nature exposed to our method of questioning.'

20th-century physicist, Werner Heisenberg

Busts of the Greek philosophers Socrates, Antisthenes, Chrysippus and Epicurus in the British Museum, London.

PHILOSOPHY BEGINS WITH QUESTIONS. THE THREE BIG ONES ARE:

What is truth?
What ought I to do? In other words, what is right – and what is wrong?
And what is beauty?

These three questions are still being wrangled over in much the same way as they were 3,000 years ago, yet many other matters have ceased to fall within the range of philosophy, which is hardly surprising, since the first philosophers considered all of nature and all of human affairs as falling within their domain of expertise.

Despite a reputation for having a love of endless discussion and a delight in disagreement, philosophers have found real answers to many questions over the years. In doing so, some subject matter has evolved in a way that it is no longer considered philosophy.

Thales of Miletus is often counted as the first philosopher, although 'scientist' would be the better term. He is remembered for his hypothesis that everything is created out of one underlying substance – which he suggested was water.

A 19th-century engraving of Thales of Miletus.

THALES AND THE MAGNETISM OF THE SOUL

Thales of Miletus (c. 625–545 BCE) has the honour of being one of the 'Seven Wise Men of the Ancient World' due to his great mathematical and astronomical understanding. Among his achievements was predicting the eclipse of 585 BCE, an almost total eclipse that took place during a battle. The soldiers of both sides stopped fighting, taking it as an omen that the gods were cross. Another story recounts how he predicted a good olive season and hired all the presses in the locale in advance. When there was a bumper crop he was able to sub-let the presses at a considerable profit.

Plato claimed that Thales fell down a well while looking up at the stars.

Plato has a less complimentary tale of Thales in the one of his dialogues, the *Theaetetus*. He describes Thales as being so busy staring up at the stars that he fell down a well.

Aristotle credits Thales with pioneering the study of 'essences', the search for defining features of entities beyond their surface attributes. Thales inspired Aristotle by studying nature, rather than starting by postulating grand theoretical entities. Thales concluded that the world was 'in essence' water, also deciding that the human soul must be a magnet, with an invisible power to move the body.

THE WAY OF TRUTH

It was Parmenides who started the Western philosophical tradition – later made famous by Plato – of asking tough questions and then not only looking for the answers but probing for definitions. His reasoning has been hailed as the dawn of a new era and formed the basis of later work by Plato.

Living, or as the historians prefer to put it, 'flourishing' in the early fifth century BCE, Parmenides of Elea tried to present the key workings of truth in the form of a long prose poem generically called by later scholars, 'On Nature', but whose main subject, appropriately enough, is 'The Way of Truth'.

The significance of the poem lies in the claim that it represents the first example of a sustained philosophical argument in the Western tradition. In his poem, Parmenides contrasts 'The Way of Truth', which leads to an unchanging and timeless universe attainable only through reflection, with 'The Way of Seeing', which is evidently much inferior, and reflects the Eastern tradition of cyclical change, light and dark, hot and cold forming each other.

The short version, though, can be summed up in just a few words: for Parmenides truth is 'what must be and cannot be otherwise'.

That truth is the wholeness of being, and reality he describes as the 'unshaken heart of well-rounded truth'.

Raphael's 16th-century 'School of Athens' fresco features a host of scholars and philosophers, including what is thought to be Parmenides, standing, in yellow.

PARMENIDES' POEM ON TRUTH FRAGMENT 2

Come now, I will tell thee
And do thou hearken to my saying and carry it away
The only two ways of search that can be thought of
The first, namely, that
It is
And that it is impossible for anything not to be,
Is the way of conviction
For truth is its companion.

The other, namely, that
It is not,
And that something must needs not be
That, I tell thee, is a wholly untrustworthy path
For you cannot know what is not
That is impossible,
Nor utter it.

Keats recreated Plato's writings in 'Ode to a Grecian Urn.'

PLATO AND THE TRUTH

Parmenides' insistence on one ultimate 'Truth' evidently greatly resonated with Plato, who developed Parmenides' ideas into his own Theory of Forms, making the older philosopher the star of no less than three of his dialogues.

One of these was named after the man himself, *The Parmenides* another was called *The Statesman*, and the third, overtly discussing the nature of truth, was called *The Sophist*.

Plato would later follow Parmenides' 'path of truth' in a bid to transform philosophy through his triad of 'Truth, Beauty, and the Good'. In Plato's dialogues, truth is a shining light revealing the world to humanity through goodness and beauty. And as Plato recreates Parmenides' poem into prose, John Keats recreates Plato's writings as a poem. Keats' insight in 'Ode to a Grecian Urn' (one of several 'Great Odes of 1819', which include 'Ode on Indolence', 'Ode on Melancholy', and the celebrated 'Ode to a Nightingale') is that 'beauty is truth, truth beauty, – that is all / Ye know on Earth, and all ye need to know.'

Zeno's paradoxes place him among the greats of Greek philosophy.

Keats, we might say was an idealist. But given the wide range of different kinds of truths being claimed, - human centred, transient truths of the past, present, and future, factual truths, truths of logic, of reasoning, and discovered through scientific investigation – many philosophers think that there needs to be a range of different, even potentially opposing, criteria for evaluating the claims.

That sounds radical, even today, but was actually something that the first philosophers had closely debated and identified too. Take Zeno, for instance. Zeno, with his paradoxes, offers another way to look at the question of truth, by showing how even the most commonsense assumptions lead us into absurdities.

Much of Zeno is about geometry and the nature of numbers – particularly the strange quantities of infinity and zero. These are mathematical concepts for which it is all too easy to offer circular, tautoglical justifications.

Zeno's paradoxes illustrate that such quick and unconsidered responses inevitably lead to contradictory and unsatisfactory conclusions.

From Zeno's Paradoxes, we recall how Achilles failed to catch up with the tortoise, as well as the 'flying arrow' being at rest.

ZENO'S ARROW PARADOX

Zeno's basic argument was that, logically, an arrow cannot fly through the air and can never reach a target, the paradox being that, in the real world, we know that it can.

The logic of the situation relies on us accepting that nothing can be in two places at once. As it flies through the air, therefore, the arrow can only be in one specific location at any given moment in time.

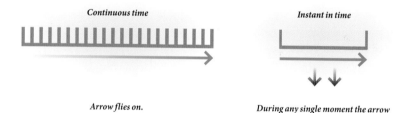

Continuous time

Arrow flies on.

Instant in time

During any single moment the arrow should be stationary and fall.

If the arrow is in one place at one particular instant, then it should fall to the ground because nothing can stand still in mid-air.

Trying to divide the flight time of the arrow up into ever smaller time periods only creates the additional problem that you can go to an infinite number of time parcels. This means that there must also be an infinite number of specific locations and, with an infinite amount of time and an infinite amount of space to cover, the arrow can surely never reach its target.

ZENO'S SUBTLE RIDDLES

The modern professor, Noson S Yanofsky, has revisited Zeno's ancient arguments, arguing that the oft-repeated mathematical responses to the issues fail to address the profound, underlying philosophical questions. The only way out of the arrow paradox, for example, is to suppose that time is made up of lots of little instants, through which the arrow jumps, as it does in a photographic sequence. That would get rid of Zeno's paradox, but at great cost elsewhere.

How so? Well, modern physics is rooted in the fact that time is continuous. All the equations have a continuous-time variable usually denoted by t. And yet, as Zeno has shown us, the notion of continuous time is illogical.

In everyday life, an infinite number of points with zero width will not stretch very far, nor will an infinite number of moments of zero duration last very long. But all modern notions of calculus, which is the basis of modern mathematics, physics and engineering, rely on such counter-intuitive properties of infinity.

Zeno of Elea.

WHAT IS TRUTH?

Truth is always something of a problematic concept in itself for philosophers. At the end of the 19th century, Nietsche wrote that 'There are no facts, only interpretations' and the notion that all truth is 'perspectival', that it is culturally and contextually bound and probably not actually 'true' either, has become the dominant philosophical meme. So first, we must start with the question of truth.

Plato says (in the *Sophist* dialogue) that something is true if it describes things as they are, a definition known as the 'correspondence theory of truth', whereas the 'coherence theory' says that something is true only when it fits within a framework of other claims, in the way, for instance, that a 'true' mathematical statement does. Over the centuries, Plato's definition has not been improved on, despite, of course, being entirely useless. What does it mean to describe things as they are, if not to simply represent the question in a slightly different form?

Writing in the 19th century, the American thinker, William James, offered as an alternative that something was true if it had useful consequences, a pragmatic approach which indeed takes the title the pragmatic theory – but even the most relativist among us have qualms at taking this approach too far.

Statue of Plato in front of the National Academy of Athens, in Greece.

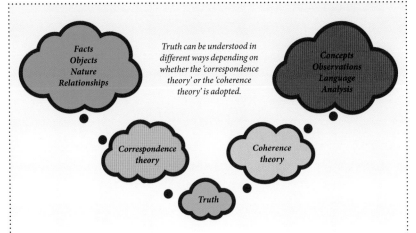

Truth can be understood in different ways depending on whether the 'correspondence theory' or the 'coherence theory' is adopted.

FRAMEWORKS FOR COMPREHENDING TRUTH

When the notion of truth is approached via the correspondence theory, truth is about facts – about what is, and what is not. It is about making sense of humanity, nature, objects, and relationships in the world around us.

Coherence theory takes a very different route. Now truth starts with human claims about the world, be they based in conceptual analysis, in language, in practical skills, or expertise. The correspondence theory is content to find just one nugget of truth – 'I think therefore I am' for example – whereas the coherence theory requires a whole system, a complete vision of ultimate Reality.

Under the pragmatic approach, of common sense and consensus, truth becomes merely another human construction, an invention, even a rule of thumb, whose sole justification is its usefulness as a guide to action.

Mohandas Gandhi understood the conflicting nature of truth.

welcome anywhere now that its values can be shown to be transitory.

In history, science, language and culture, truths change. Research revealing new facts that are held up for inspection,are liable to be revised as more new research creates more new facts, and are subject to controversy when they are disputed. Truth is unwelcome because it has a coercive power: it cannot be denied. True facts impose themselves on the world.

The truth can be constricting, and confining just as easily as it can be liberating and enlightening, a point the great 20th-century liberation philosopher, Mohandas Gandhi, made when he wrote in *The Story of My Experiments With Truth*:

'The seeker after truth should be humbler than the dust. The world crushes the dust under its feet, but the seeker after truth should so humble himself that even the dust could crush him.

'Only then, and not till then, will he have a glimpse of truth.'

Sometimes it seems today as if Truth has been handcuffed and led into a padded cell where its claims are ridiculed or at least limited to rather particular, well-defined situations.

The perspective of a nobler Truth as enlightenment, insight, and wisdom, has been lost, relegated to the province of religion. It seems that it is no longer

THE REGIME OF TRUTH

'Each society has its regime of truth, its general politics, of truth: that is, the types of discourse that it accepts and makes function as true.

The intellectual par excellence used to be the writer: as a universal consciousness, a free subject, he was counterposed to those intellectuals who were merely competent instances in the service of the State or Capital-technicians, magistrates, teachers. Since the time when each individual's specific activity began to serve as the basis for politicisation, the threshold of writing, as the sacralising mark of the intellectual, has disappeared. And it has become possible to develop lateral connections across different forms of knowledge and from one focus of politicisation to another. Magistrates and psychiatrists, doctors and social workers, laboratory technicians and sociologists have become able to participate, both within their own fields and through mutual exchange and support, in a global process of politicisation of intellectuals.'

Michel Foucault

'Truth and Power' in *The Foucault Reader* (1984)

French philosopher Michel Foucault.

WHAT OUGHT I TO DO?

Whatever David Hume might have meant by his famous dictum, 'an is does not and cannot imply an ought', Foucault shows that questions about what 'is' are, in practice, often determined by other, unexamined, assumptions about what 'ought' to be the case. The Ancient philosophers were right, in other words, to put ethics at the start of their search for wisdom.

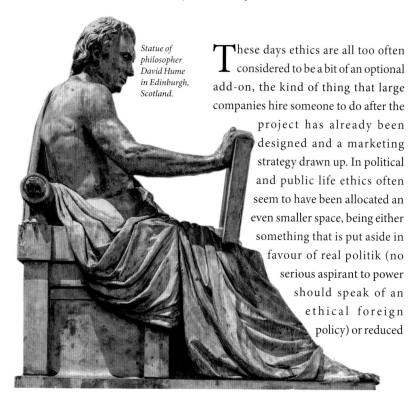

Statue of philosopher David Hume in Edinburgh, Scotland.

These days ethics are all too often considered to be a bit of an optional add-on, the kind of thing that large companies hire someone to do after the project has already been designed and a marketing strategy drawn up. In political and public life ethics often seem to have been allocated an even smaller space, being either something that is put aside in favour of real politik (no serious aspirant to power should speak of an ethical foreign policy) or reduced

Karl Marx agreed with Plato's practical view of good and evil.

to the trappings of family life for an electoral photo opportunity.

But for the Ancient philosophers ethics were the key to everything else. It can be hard for us today, living in an age of technology, dependent for every need on human invention and ingenuity, to really appreciate just why this is the area that the Ancient philosophers considered of prime importance. As the Greeks also left plenty of ruminations on other topics, history tends to rewrite their concerns. Nonetheless, Plato had no doubt that, as Marx would later have applauded, the study of good and evil is essentially a practical study.

In Plato's dialogues, the source of goodness is wisdom, and 'the good' is described as a light that reveals truth. No one does evil, says Plato, except out of ignorance, which is reassuring – but is it really true?

DOING THE RIGHT THING

The claim is that doing something wrong makes someone less perfect, less harmonious, and who would knowingly do that to themselves? Well, Plato thought it was unthinkable... Aristotle, who normally disagreed with his mentor on most things, accepts the reasoning too – suggesting that the path to ethical health is a series of fine judgements in search of moderation: not too much wine, nor too many slave boys.

Yet, while Plato ends up with an ascetic class of Philosopher-Guardians, eating simply and shunning plays and music, Aristotle's hero is a rather monstrous fellow. See how he describes his 'Magnanimous Man' opposite. In recent years, Aristotle's view, dubbed 'Virtue ethics', has had something of a revival on ethics courses!

Plato's and Aristotle's approaches (at least as received down the ages) are actually quite a contrast with the Stoic and Eastern traditions

Aristotle believed in moderation in all things.

epitomised by Confucius and the Taoists that consider 'the good life' as harmonising with nature and the 'times'.

Both approaches avoid the 'right/wrong' duality of Western ethics in recognising that everything contains elements of both good and bad – which is why ethical decision making can seem so hard!

But Aristotle's account later suited the new religious authorities in the West better, and indeed Plato also rejected such relativism, preferring to firmly and categorically split good and evil asunder. It was this conviction that endeared their writings to the Christian Church throughout the medieval period.

'... Such, then, is the magnanimous man; the man who goes to excess and is vulgar exceeds, as has been said, by spending beyond what is right. For on small objects of expenditure he spends much and displays a tasteless showiness; because he thinks he is admired for these things, and where he ought to spend much he spends little and where little, much. The niggardly man on the other hand will fall short in everything, and after spending the greatest sums will spoil the beauty of the result for a trifle, and whatever he is doing he will hesitate and consider how he may spend least, and lament even that, and think he is doing everything on a bigger scale than he ought... '

Aristotle describes his ideal or 'Magnanimous Man' in the *Nicomachean Ethics*

Plato (left) walks with Aristotle in Raphael's 'School of Athens' fresco.

WISDOM OF THE EAST

However the writings of the Greeks may have been reinterpreted, and for whatever reasons, the Ancient Chinese thinkers were unambiguously focused on practical advice for rulers – on how to run the kingdom – and for the ruled on how to live.

Confucius, Lao Tzu, Mencius and Chuang Tzu offer timeless insights into ethics and social policy. Chuang Tzu, for instance, sees a bit of good in everything. One of the key themes of Chuang Tzu (369–286 BCE), is the unity of all things, and the dynamic interplay of opposites. 'Good' and 'bad', Chuang Tzu points out, are inter-related and interchangeable. Like everything else.

Buddha statues at Seema Malakaya temple, Colombo, Sri Lanka.

For example, he says, if killing is always wrong, is it wrong to kill a hare if this is the only way to save yourself from starving? Surely not. Is it, however, still always wrong to kill another human being? But what if that human being is a robber intent on killing a family? Surely it is then not wrong to kill him? Chuang Tzu, the historical figure, the book (written by several sources) and the poetry, as well as philosophical arguments, have always been highly popular throughout the East. Buddhism draws on his teaching that suffering is mainly a result of refusing to accept 'what is', while Zen philosophy reflects his love of paradoxes or 'koans'.

Within China, his message of nonconformity and freedom is credited with helping to 'unshackle' the Chinese mind from some of the effects of over-rigid Confucianism.

CHUANG TZU'S BUTTERFLY DREAM

'Once I, Chuang Chou, dreamed I was a butterfly and was happy as a butterfly. I was conscious that I was quite pleased with myself, but I did not know that I was Chou. Suddenly I awoke, and there I was, visibly Chou. I do not know whether it was Chou dreaming he was a butterfly, or the butterfly dreaming it was Chou.'

'The Butterfly Dream', one of Chuang Tzu's most famous arguments, seeks to show the relativity of all judgements. His conclusion was that we should strive to transcend the world of distinctions.

Chuang Tzu dreams of butterflies in this 16th-century ink-on-silk painting.

THE GREAT SAGE

Confucius (551– 479 BCE) was the essence of the ancient Chinese sage, a social philosopher, and a dedicated teacher of men. It is said that altogether he had 3,000 disciples of whom '72 of them were influential'. (Not quite the same as Facebook likes, but not bad for the time...)

Modesty being a virtue, Confucius liked to present himself as a transmitter who invented nothing and, indeed, he puts the greatest emphasis on learning from your elders and betters – in his case, absorbing and understanding the wisdom of the ancient sages.

His teachings, preserved in *The Analects*, are part of the underlying bedrock of much of subsequent Chinese speculation on education, government and virtuous behavior. Confucius's position in Chinese culture can indeed properly be compared with Socrates and Plato's in the West.

Seen from the Western perspective, however, Confucian wisdom appears distorted by being reduced to aphorisms or moral maxims.

In the process, the context and associations that gave rise to the maxims are lost, and so the depth of the influence of Confucianism becomes hard for Western philosophy to understand.

Confucius' ethical and social views largely revolve around the concepts of rites or rituals which operate within a notion of common humanity.

The Analects of Confucius in the Museum of Far Eastern Antiquities, Stockholm, Sweden.

The system of ritual rules in Confucius' time came originally from the Western Zhou dynasty (1066 BCE–771 BCE) and had lasted for 300 years.

Confucius was concerned to see that, over time, the power of the royal house of Zhou had declined, while that of the feuding princes of rival states had risen.

He saw upturned traditions as contributing to many social woes. Confucius shared with Socrates the aim of having true wisdom recognised as being more than simply a shallow, surface appearance.

Just as music did not consist of the mere beating of drums and the tinkling of bells, Confucius thought that both ritual and music arose from, and created, a state of mind. This was a state of God-fearing piety in the performance of ritual and a state of happiness and harmony in the performance of music.

Performing rituals thus nourishes and strengthens good character.

This is the argument better known to Western philosophers as 'Virtue Ethics', and has been historically associated with the great Aristotle.

King Wu of the Western Zhou Dynasty.

CONFUCIUS' POLITE SOCIETY

Confucius had great respect for traditional rites such as marriage and funeral ceremonies, which he seems to have seen as the building blocks of a virtuous society. He insists that any problem was not in the rites themselves but with the people who either no longer performed them, or performed them without sincerity.

Confucius believed that nothing that anyone did was truly worthwhile unless it was done with the right motive and intention.

For him, the importance of an action depends on the attitude with which it is performed. You should believe in what you do, and always do it for the right reasons, always in the right frame of mind.

For example, it is essential to truly feel reverence for the spirits when carrying out the rites of mourning, to genuinely feel grief for the deceased. So when asked about the justification for spending on traditional ceremonies, Confucius replied to his followers:

'An important question indeed. In rituals or ceremonies, be thrifty rather than extravagant, and in funerals, be deeply sorrowful rather than shallow in your sentiment.'

This focus on people's true beliefs and motives is actually quite democratic – and contrasted with a rival approach of the time called Legalism. Legalism advocated bringing the masses into line by a severe system of penal law. As Confucius said:

'Lead the people with governmental measures and regulate them by law and punishment, and they will avoid wrongdoing but will have no sense of honour and shame. Lead them with virtue and regulate them by the rules of propriety, and they will have a sense of shame.'

Confucius Temple in Taipei City, China.

CONFUCIAN MUSIC

Confucius not only said wise and interesting things, he also sang them and accompanied himself on a 'qin', which was a stringed instrument rather like a zither. His songs were mainly the odes of the Classic of Poetry.

This image of the philosopher-musician became firmly established later through popular accounts of his life. Confucius had clear ideas about the importance of music. He said: 'Let a man be stimulated by poetry, established by the rules of propriety, perfected by music.'

For Confucius, music not only reflects the feelings of man, but it can also mould man's character. This is because the harmony which is the essence of music can find its way into the hidden recesses of the mind and soul.

Emperor Huizong of Song, listening to the qin

Confucius, like Socrates, insisted that human nature is essentially virtuous: initially quiet and calm, but disturbed by the external world, which presents it with temptations and things to desire.

When the desires are not properly controlled, we lose our true selves and the principle of reason is clouded. From this state soon arises all the evils of society: rebellion, disobedience, cunning and deceit, and general immorality. In short, as English philosopher Thomas Hobbes would say 2000 years later, chaos.

Mencius saw human nature as being basically virtuous.

MENCIUS BACKS UP THE MASTER'S ARGUMENTS

Mencius (371–289 BCE), known as 'the Second Sage' of Confucianism, argued that, if human nature is studied in terms of life, then it follows that the nature of a dog is the same as that of an ox, and the nature of an ox is the same as that of a man.

Instead, he explained human nature in terms of its moral quality, declaring that it is originally good. He pointed out that a person who sees a child about to fall into a well rushes to save the child. This is not to gain favour with the child's parents, or to seek the approbation of his neighbours, or for fear of blame should he fail to rescue the child. It is due to the spontaneous response of human nature.

From this it follows that sympathy, repentance, courtesy, and judgement on what is right and wrong are the four beginnings of humanity, righteousness, propriety and wisdom. Mencius maintained that these virtues do not come to us from outside but are rooted in human nature. Unfortunately, many people cannot develop them.

Thus Mencius sighed: 'When persons' fowls and dogs are lost, they know enough to seek them again; but if they lose their human heart/mind, they do not know to seek for it.'

SOOTHING MUSIC

When Thomas Hobbes was writing in the 17th century, he covered a range of subjects, including the sciences, but it was for his contributions to political philosophy and social science that he became best known, living as he did through the chaos of the English Civil War.

Thomas Hobbes lived through one of the most traumatic periods in English history.

Hobbes offered no magic recipe for restoring good sense to the greedy masses, but Chinese sage Confucius had one idea, which is music.

Music, he says, springs from and reaches into the inner movement of the soul, and good music can help to restore calm and order to its disturbed workings.

'Therefore, the superior man tries to create harmony in the human heart by a rediscovery of human nature, and tries to promote music as a means to the perfection of human culture. When such music prevails and the people's minds are led towards the right ideals and aspirations, we may see the appearance of a great nation.'

So thought Confucius, perhaps rather optimistically. Surely Confucius would not recognise modern music in the same vein. Rap music used by tank crews in combat, as apparently it routinely was during the Gulf War, to inflame the killing zeal, would be totally alien.

For Confucius, musical training was the most effective method for changing the moral character of man and keeping society calm and in good order.

LIFE OF THE MASTER

Confucius was born in Qufu in Lu State, now part of present-day Shandong Province. As a child, Confucius is said to have enjoyed putting ritual vases on the sacrifice table. His first role was as a minor administrative manager in the State of Lu but he soon rose to the position of Justice Minister. He earned a reputation for fairness, politeness and love of learning. He studied ritual with the Daoist Master Lao Dan, music with Chang Hong, and the lute with Music-master Xiang.

When he was about 50, he gave up his political career in Lu, and began a 12-year journey around China, seeking the 'Way' and trying unsuccessfully to convert different rulers to his political beliefs.

Returning home, he spent the remainder of his life teaching and editing the ancient classics. Considered as a 'throneless king', he tried to share his experiences with his disciples and to transmit the old wisdom to the later generations. He died aged 72.

Confucius was a politician before becoming a teacher.

TAO, AND TAOISM

If they disagreed on music, (Plato wanted it banned), Confucius and Plato certainly belong in the same camp on many issues, but it is another great Chinese sage, Lao Tzu (c. 6th century BCE), who is traditionally viewed as the Eastern twin of Plato.

Lao Tzu was the author of the classic of Taoism the *Tao Te Ching*, or the *The Way and Its Power*.

Its central message is that everything follows certain patterns – 'the way'. Humans should also 'follow the way', and yield to the times and influences. The lessons here are not as passive and negative as many assume. It is part of the philosophy that 'the way' applies to very small as much as to the great things. The Tao is probably the central idea in Chinese philosophy, and its echoes are there in Ancient Greek texts, too. Despite that, conventional Western philosophy refuses to acknowledge it as a serious historical theory.

The text of the *I Ching* (c. 900 BCE), or *Book of Changes*, that Confucius himself says contains: '… the profoundest secrets of the universe; and the power of exciting the various motions of the universe…' is essentially an investigation of the Tao, and how to understand the world.

Lao Tzu statue at the Yuanxuan Taoist temple, Guangzhou, China.

Lao Tzu sets out for the border riding an ox.

LAO TZU SUMS IT ALL UP WITH A FEW WELL-CHOSEN WORDS

The story goes that one day Lao Tzu was unhappy with China and wanted to leave it to travel, setting off on an ox, or possibly a water buffalo.

At the frontier, a guard recognised him as the great sage and refused to let him pass unless he first recorded all his wisdom on parchment. Because of, or perhaps despite, being indubitably very wise, Lao Tzu managed to do this in just a few weeks, producing a volume of a little over 5,000 Chinese characters. An early chapter reads:

Something amorphous and consummate existed before Heaven and Earth.
Solitude! Vast! Standing alone, unaltering. Going everywhere, yet unthreatened.
It can be considered the Mother of the World.
I don't know its name, so I designate it, 'Tao'.
Compelled to consider it, name it 'The Great.'

SO WHAT IS THE TAO?

. .like a bowl, it may be used, but is never emptied, it is bottomless, the ancestor of all things, it blunts sharpness, it unties knots, it softens the light, it becomes one with the dusty world – deep and still, it exists for ever.

Lao Tzu, Tao Te Ching, *fourth verse*

These days, Lao Tzu is still revered in China as one of the great sages, yet he is barely acknowledged in the West. Many reference works on philosophy omit him entirely. This is difficult to justify given that he was so worshipped by so many devotees.

For those who place Lao Tzu somewhere between immortality and complete non-existence, he was born in the 6th century BCE at Juren in the State of Chu.

Legend has it that when he became disillusioned with life in China and attempted to leave, the sentry who stopped him was won over by his philosophy and left with him, never to be seen again.

Of course, they left behind Lao Tzu's complete works in the form of the *Tao Te Ching*. The earliest manuscript copies known date back to the second century BCE, but for many it was assumed to have a divine origin (like the Bible), with Lao Tzu regarded not merely as an author, or even a prophet, but as an immortal.

Chinese philosophies, in particular, regard thinking and acting as two aspects of one activity – two sides of the same coin. T'ai Chi, the 'ultimate reality' martial art, is a combination of mind and matter, and the aim is to align yourself with the Tao.

The aim of Tai Chi is to align yourself with the Tao.

Lao Tzu stone sculpture at the foot of Mount Quingyuan in Fujian, China.

TAO TE CHING

Whatever its origins, the *Tao Te Ching* represents a repository of enormously powerful ideas, expressed with poetic simplicity.

Human beings are born soft and flexible; yet when they die that are stiff and hard...
Plants sprout soft and delicate, yet when they die they are withered and dry...
Thus the hard and stiff are disciples of death, the soft and flexible are disciples of life,
Thus an inflexible army is not victorious, an unbending tree will break.
The stiff and massive will be lessened, the soft and fluid will increase.

AESTHETICS, ART AND BEAUTY

Philosophers agree very little on 'beauty', which is not in itself a very unusual thing. After all, they agree very little on tables, on the colour of snow, and so on... Some say assessing beauty is an aesthetic judgement, others say not. The debate rages on.

Some say beauty is both capable of definition and 'objective', like Plato with his 'ideal form' of 'the beautiful'; others say it is entirely subjective and beneath serious consideration. If it is the latter, then it is purely a matter of emotional response.

The hallmarks of beauty, from classical times, were held to be harmony, proportion and unity. The term 'aesthetic' is derived from the Greek word for perception, and originally applied to things that are perceived by the senses as opposed to being objects of thought. The narrower and more recent meaning of the term in the philosophy of art is that it involves the criticism of taste and the appreciation of the beautiful.

And beauty was linked by the ancient philosophers to goodness. The link, however, is part of a tripod – there is also skilfulness. Beauty, in this sense, cannot come from whirling a bucket of paint around, whatever Jackson Pollock might have thought his art demonstrated.

Greek art involved harmony and proportion but also encompassed tragedy as in this depiction of a fallen Trojan warrior.

BEAUTY AND VIRTUE

Arete is the ancient Greek term denoting excellence, goodness, and exceptionality of any kind, especially of the supposedly manly virtues, such as the ability to kill lots of enemies in battle. The virtues of arete are decidedly militaristic, thus, even Socrates – recently reinvented as almost a secular saint – in fact loudly boasts of his courage in battle (rather than of his private contemplations) when he wants to prove his goodness to the Athenians in the dialogue, *The Apology*.

The Greek phrase, *kalos kai agathos* ('beautiful and good'), was the standard description of the Homeric heroes. Plato's most important account of the nature of beauty is credited not to Socrates, but to the wise woman, Diotima. She advises a youthful Socrates in *The Symposium* that:

'You should use the things of this world as rungs in a ladder. You start by loving one attractive body and step up to two; from there to the beauty of people's activities, from there to the beauty of intellectual endeavours and from there you ascend to that final intellectual endeavour which is no more and no less than the study of that beauty, so that you finally recognise true beauty.'

Diotima of Mantinea.

A WOMAN DEFINES BEAUTY

Remarkably, Plato credits his most famous theory, the Theory of the Forms or Ideas, to a priestess and philosopher called Diotima, thereby putting a woman at the heart of Western philosophy.

Despite the scope of her theory being clearly universal, she is often credited only with influencing Plato's views on love, but that, I suppose, is still an important topic! This is her insight on love in Plato's *The Symposium*:

> *'According to Greek mythology, humans were originally created with four arms, four legs and a head with two faces. Fearing their power, Zeus split them into two separate parts, condemning them to spend their lives in search of their other halves... "Love" is the name for our pursuit of wholeness, for our desire to be complete.'*

Diotima is at the heart of Western philosophy.

Or recall the challenge to the teachings of Confucius in ancient China. To defend and justify elaborate funeral traditions, as Confucius recommended, Mencius replied:

> *'In ancient times there was no burial of one's parents. When a man's parent died, he simply threw the body into a ditch. When he later passed by, what he saw was that the body was being eaten by the foxes or bitten by the gnats or flies...*
>
> *'He could not bear the sight. The feeling of the heart flew out to his face.*
>
> *'He then hurried home and came back with baskets and a spade for covering up the body. If the covering up of a human body was the right thing for primitive man, it is quite right today for a filial son or man of ren to prepare the funeral for his parents.'*

In this response, Mencius links ethics with aesthetic repugnance, thus emphasising the importance of the third pillar of philosophy – the study of the beautiful.

Plato directly linked beauty to truth, generating the historic philosophical trilogy: truth, beauty and goodness. But what is beauty's relation to truth and virtue? Mathematicians are happy to see certain relationships between numbers as more beautiful than others, while the equation of virtue and beauty touches something deep in the human psyche.

As David Hume put it in *Of the Standard of Taste* (1757): 'It appears then, that, amidst all the variety and caprice of taste, there are certain general principles of approbation or blame, whose influence a careful eye may trace in all operations of the mind.'

THE SEARCH FOR BEAUTY

Arthur Schopenhauer

In his Enquiry Concerning Beauty, Order, Harmony, Design *(1725), Francis Hutcheson (1694–1746) argued that recognising an object as beautiful was a matter of distinguishing its special aesthetic qualities from factual or empirical ones. The beauty of an object lay in its capacity to affect an observer in some particular way.*

Different kinds of arts (genres) produce different responses: comedy from tragedy, exotic art from music, and so on.

This suggests that a person's emotional or aesthetic response will depend not only on the object itself, but on which aspect of it the observer is focussing. To feel beauty, as the German philosopher, Schopenhauer says, requires recognition that: 'each thing has its own characteristic beauty, not only everything organic which expresses itself in the unity of an individual being, but also everything inorganic and formless, and even every manufactured article.'

But Schopenhauer also went to argue that there is something universal that encompasses all of the particular instances of beauty: 'In such contemplation the particular thing becomes at once the Idea of its species, and the perceiving individual becomes pure subject of knowledge.'

Similarly, the English art critic John Ruskin (1819–1900) thought he distinguished a spiritual core to all the objects of beauty.

BEAUTY AND LOGIC

In his dry *Critique of Judgement* (1790), Kant discusses beauty, concluding that beauty depends on appearance and within that on form and design. In visual art, he said, it is not the colours but the pattern that the colours make; in music, the relation between the sounds, not timbre or pitch that matter.

Such accounts of art were highly influential in the 19th century, but the 20th brought a greater concern with matter over form and a challenge to the idea of art and beauty as moral concepts. Even David Hume, ever the humbugger of value judgements, allowed those of beauty as arising from sentiment yet still deserving, on the whole, of universal acceptance. Nonetheless, over the years a very different approach to philosophy would increasingly predominate: that of logic and mathematics.

Immanuel Kant, Prussian philosopher.

CHAPTER 2
THE GOLDEN AGE
OF PHILOSOPHY

'... Let us proceed to distribute the elementary forms, which have now been created in idea, among the four elements. To earth, then, let us assign the cubical form; for earth is the most immovable of the four and the most plastic of all bodies, and that which has the most stable bases must of necessity be of such a nature!'

Plato, *The Timæus*

SOL

LVNA

TERRA

THE PLATONIC SOLIDS

The grand theatre of the golden age of philosophy is set in Ancient Athens and the stars are indisputably Plato and Aristotle, even if many of the supporting cast of 'Greek philosophers' were not Greek at all, but African or Turkish or Italian.

The Mediterranean was a one big melting pot for ideas and cultures. From Elea, in Italy, came the school of Eleatic philosophy led by Parmenides, a philosopher and poet. Its best-known member was Zeno, author of several paradoxes of time and motion.

From Babylon and Alexandria came the maths that built the pyramids, and the whole method of logic and systematic proof that science and philosophy have drawn on ever since. Euclid's *Elements*, in which he sets out definitions and clear-as-day assumptions in order to demonstrate a wealth of geometrical facts, was for a thousand years the epitome of pure knowledge, as desired by philosophers.

From the island principality of Samos, came Pythagoras with his conviction that all knowledge was ultimately about 'numbers'. The name may not mean much to you other than perhaps as a distant, memory of maths at school, yet if it has often been said that the whole of Western philosophy is footnotes to Plato, it should also be recognised that the whole of Plato is footnotes to Pythagoras.

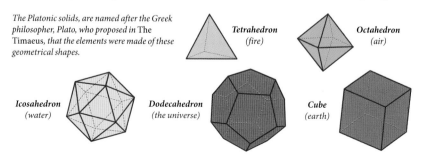

The Platonic solids, are named after the Greek philosopher, Plato, who proposed in The Timaeus, *that the elements were made of these geometrical shapes.*

Tetrahedron
(fire)

Octahedron
(air)

Icosahedron
(water)

Dodecahedron
(the universe)

Cube
(earth)

PLATO'S CRIB SHEET

Plato, the most famous philosopher of them all, is a subtle writer who drew on many sources. Sometimes he cheerfully drew on two opposing views, leaving later scholars guessing which one he really believed. Nonetheless, it is through Plato that we are introduced to the Pythagorean ideas (then incredible) that key human concepts are built into our minds; that men and women are equal; that the book of nature is written (as Newton later put it) in mathematics. Pythagoras' ideas that property should be held in common, and that adherents should live and eat communally all reappear in *The Republic* as Plato's recommended lifestyle for The Guardians.

Here's Plato's crib sheet:

- In *The Meno*, Pythagoras' view of how learning is really recollection appears, as the 'slave boy' recalls the geometrical theorem that bears Pythagoras' name.
- In *The Gorgias*, the Pythagorean doctrine that the better one knows something, the more one becomes like it is trailed.
- In *The Timaeus*, an account straight out of Pythagoras describes the universe in terms of musical harmonies, and matter as being made up of geometrical shapes, notably triangles. Five shapes represent the four elements (fire, earth, air and water) and the dodecahedron represents the universe.
- In *The Phaedo* it states that 'philosophy is a preparation for death and immortality'.

PREPARE TO DIE

In line with the Pythagorean conviction that life is preparation for dying well, it is significant that Plato's famous closing drama of Socrates inviting his friends to sit with him as he drinks poison is presented as an uplifting tale and not the weepy 'tragedy' that modern-day writers insist it must have been. Who is right?

One fact does sit oddly with today's bitter condemnations of the Athenians who ordered Socrates' death: Socrates was offered many alternatives, from recanting his views to leaving Athens, making his final drink more like a suicide act than a real execution.

Or is it a political statement? Plato's family was politically ambitious, and *The Republic* is not only a central text in western philosophical thought, but a political manifesto. Through it, Plato condemns the rule of the unwise, and promotes a ruling class based on merit. Philosophical merit, of course. The dialogue is, like all Plato's dialogues,

19th-century illustration of the death of Socrates.

written in the form of a little playlet, starring Socrates, but it seems highly unlikely that the historical Socrates really thought such a thing.

It's important to bear in mind when reading Plato that nothing should be taken at face value. Although in the dialogue, *The Republic*, we have an apparently clear condemnation of poetry and even sex (children are to be produced in the ideal state in a more controlled way), in another one, called *The Symposium*, sex and music are both praised as providing alternative routes to the highest possible knowledge – notably that of beauty and truth.

PLATO'S POLITICAL ADVENTURE

Plato (427–347 BCE) was born, studied, taught, and died in Athens, although he did spend several years visiting Greek cities in Africa and Italy, absorbing Pythagorean notions and then, in 387 BCE, he returned to Athens.

Plato apparently lived to the age of 80.

of philosophy in Athens, generally considered the first 'university'. Years later, he is reported to have died in his sleep at the age of 80, after enjoying a student's wedding feast.

One exception to this scholarly existence was when he visited Syracuse in the 360s to advise the new king, Dionysius II. This may have been an attempt to put the ideals of *The Republic* into practice. If so, it was disastrous. Plato fell out with the king, and only just managed to escape with his life.

One ripping yarn has it that he was captured by pirates and held for ransom. Whether that is true or not, the second half of his life is far more placid, Plato establishing the famous 'Academy' for the study

IT'S NOT GEOMETRY

Although Socrates stars in Plato's dialogues, his life and works are a bit of a mystery.
It is, however, only the Socrates described by Plato that matters philosophically.
Plato illustrates his own views via Socrates, and there are other clues about what
Plato really thought. Above the doorway to his famous Academy it was boldly written:

LET NO ONE IGNORANT OF MATHEMATICS ENTER HERE

That looks rather prescriptive – might even exclude me – but bear in mind the story of Socrates teasing out Pythagoras' theorem from an apparently ignorant slave boy. This is more than an interesting social comment, because the maths Plato talks about involves being able to reason methodically and to draw conclusions.

The modern thinker, Peter Hubral, says that the word 'mathematics' is misleading. The correct Greek term is 'geometria'. Although that looks like geometry, and many philosophers have waxed lyrical on the

Thoth, the ancient Egyptian god of wisdom and knowledge, sometimes shown with the head of an ibis.

Greek philosophers' discovery of 'geometry', Hubral says that geometry and geometría are quite different. Not so much chalk and cheese as cheddar and cheese.

But let me explain. In Plato's best known dialogue, *The Republic*, geometría is introduced as that which is pursued for the sake of the knowledge of what 'eternally exists'.

Plato says that this kind of geometría was discovered by someone called Thoth. Thoth, or Theuth, was the Egyptian god of knowledge, one of the top gods of the Egyptian pantheon. He was depicted as a man with the head of an ibis

THE EGYPTIAN GOD THOTH

'*At the Egyptian city of Naucratis, there was a famous old god, whose name was Theuth; the bird which is called the Ibis is sacred to him, and he was the inventor of many arts, such as arithmetic and calculation and geometry and astronomy and draughts and dice, but his great discovery was the use of letters.*'

Socrates
speaking in The Phaedrus *dialogue by Plato*

Thoth was also depicted as a baboon.

or a baboon. This reference to Theuth illustrates two things: the importance of the Egyptian ideas, and that the kind of logic and maths the first philosophers were talking about is not the kind that people today imagine them to have been developing.

When Plato describes Meno's slave boy 'deducing' Pythagoras's theorem, he is doing schoolbook geometry, yes, but the point of the dialogue is not to tell the world how to measure the length of a hypotenuse. It is to illustrate that we all have access to the world of timeless truths. In this case, the truths are mathematical ones.

WHO WAS PYTHAGORAS?

Plato argues for the Pythagorean view of the universe, in which the heavens were expected to exhibit timeless perfection and the geometry of the gods. This is why the ancients thought it only right that the stars should circle the Earth on perfect crystal spheres, making music as they turned.

However, Plato deplores overly literal interpretations of the cosmic geometry, regretting that 'the great mass of mankind' doggedly regard the geometrical and mechanical descriptions of phenomena 'as the sole causes of all things'. Such causes are 'incapable of any plan or intelligence for any purpose'.

Plato speaks up for Pythagoras because Pythagoras was, and is, often misrepresented. Over the centuries he has been depicted as a rogue who was not a true philosopher, but rather a charlatan, part priest, part conjurer, who wore a strange cultish outfit (a white robe, trousers and a coronet) and, worst of all, wrote poetry.

Pythagoras with an attentive audience in Raphael's 'School of Athens' fresco.

LIFE OF PYTHAGORAS

The stories about Pythagoras may well all be true, but are misleading nonetheless.

Not only did he make important contributions to music and astronomy, metaphysics, natural philosophy, politics and theology, but he also brought the concepts of

PITAGORA

Pythagoras' followers formed what would nowadays be described as a cult.

reincarnation, heaven and hell to Western Europe, declaring that the doctrines were a personal revelation to himself. It seems he was born on the island of Samos, just off the coast of Turkey. Driven from Samos in 529 BCE when the tyrant Polycrates declared him a subversive, he went to Italy, where he established a school of philosophy at Croton in the south, as well as a monastic order based on practising vegetarianism, poverty and chastity.

The crucial event in Pythagoras' life appears to have been visiting Egypt, where he avidly soaked up all the new wisdom, especially the mathematical sort that the priests and architects behind the pyramids had developed. Later, as a prisoner of war, he went to Babylon and was introduced to another rich tradition of geometrical and mathematical wisdom.

The Pythagoreans thought 'true knowledge' had to be about things that did not change. They wanted objects of thought that were pure, fixed and eternal. And they thought they had found them in the abstract world of numbers. If you've ever wondered what Plato had in mind when he talked about those mysterious 'heavenly Forms', well, numbers are a good place to start.

PYTHAGORAS COUNTS FROM 1 TO 10

It is said that Pythagoras invented the word 'philosophy', or love of wisdom, to cover their investigation of the mysteries of the other world of numbers.

The Pythagorean approach echoes the writings of the Chinese sage, Lao Tzu, who wrote in his *Tao Te Ching*: 'From the Tao comes one, from one comes two, from two comes three, and from three comes the ten thousand things.'

The Pythagorean theory, also known as 'The Monad', is clearly drawn from the Eastern idea of Yin and Yang.

In the Monad, two opposite powers separate and recombine to form everything else in the rest of the universe.

It starts with 'Unity' or the number One. Geometrically, it is a dimensionless point. For the Pythagoreans, as for today's most sophisticated cosmologists with their theories of the Big Bang, a singularity is the source of all things. For today's scientists, however, splitting a singularity causes a tremendous explosion. For the Pythagoreans it only results in two points, and two points make a line. Nonetheless, since the number Two is imperfect, it creates the possibility of division.

The number Three was called 'The Whole' because it combines One and Two, and allows for a beginning, middle, and end. Geometrically, Three is the first shape – a triangle. The number Four, represents the square, and was considered perfect. With Four, the realm of physical bodies has been reached as a three dimensional

In Chinese philosophy, yin-yang, describes opposite forces as complementary, interconnected, and dependent on each other.

figure (a pyramid) can be constructed from just four points.

The numbers Five and Six were both called 'Marriage' as they combined Two and Three, considered the male and female numbers.

The number Seven was called 'The Virgin', as it cannot be created by any other numbers multiplying, and the number Eight is the first 'cube' number, being 2x2x2.

The number Nine was called 'The Horizon' for no better reason than it

is the last number before 'The Decad' or number Ten.

Ten contains all the other numbers and can be constructed in lots of interesting ways, such as by adding 1, 2, 3 and 4; or by cubing 1 and 3 and then adding them together.

Because it can be created from various prime numbers, Ten also contains all musical and arithmetical proportions, and represents the universe. The Pythagoreans considered it a deity and swore devoutly by it.

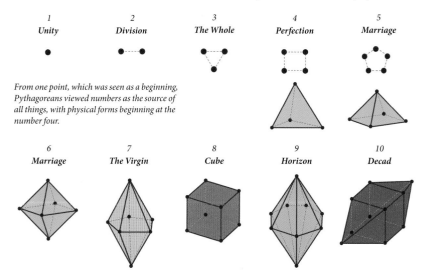

1	2	3	4	5
Unity	*Division*	*The Whole*	*Perfection*	*Marriage*

From one point, which was seen as a beginning, Pythagoreans viewed numbers as the source of all things, with physical forms beginning at the number four.

6	7	8	9	10
Marriage	*The Virgin*	*Cube*	*Horizon*	*Decad*

LEGENDS AND SECRETS

Pythagoras never actually wrote anything down, so most of what we think we know about what he actually believed comes from third parties who were often keen to tell tall tales and gossip about the slightly odd, perhaps sinister, cult.

There are many strange stories about the Pythagoreans. Some record Pythagoras' extraordinary feats, including legends in which he:

- Predicted that an approaching ship would carry a dead body.
- Bit a serpent to death.
- Addressed the river Cosas and it replied, 'Hail Pythagoras!'

One sad story tells of one of Pythagoras' students, Hippasus, who was cast out to sea to drown after giving away to the 'uninitiated' the awkward fact that some geometrical qualities (such as the square root of 2) cannot be expressed at all as whole numbers. This kind of fact was deeply troubling for the Pythagoreans, so they preferred to keep it secret.

Pythagoreans were instructed to get up before, and celebrate, sunrise.

Heraclitus as portrayed in Raphael's 'School of Athens' fresco.

SEARCHING FOR CERTAINTY

Not everyone was a fan. Heraclitus describes Pythagoras as a charlatan, who stole other people's ideas and passed them off to his followers as his own. He calls him a thieving jackdaw, whose craft is not wisdom but deceit.

Heraclitus thought that in order for something to be able to change, it had already to contain within it the seeds of what it would become.

For example, water is not hard, like a rock, but it is when it becomes ice. Thus, water is both hard and not hard, depending on the temperature.

In *On Divination* (44 BCE), Cicero adds to the stock of Pythagorean misinformation by explaining that the rule instructing Pythagoreans to 'abstain from beans' was instigated because beans 'have a flatulent tendency inimical to the pursuit of mental tranquillity.'

This, however, was an unkind joke on the sect, but one now confused with historical fact. Pythagoras was instructing his followers not to gamble, which in those days involved drawing beans from a jar.

LEARNING THE RULES

According to Iamblichus, writing in the third century, the junior monks were not allowed to see Pythagoras and listened to him talking only from behind a veil. The lectures are supposed to have consisted (like the advice from the Delphic Oracle) of brief sayings or maxims.

Some of the sayings that the novices had to learn were more like rules, and rules, of course, are the first things that we all must learn. Pythagoras' rules were, naturally, every bit as strange as you would expect and included:

This plate shows King Aigeus of Athens seeking a prophecy from the Delphic Oracle.

- Do not help to unload a burden, but do help to load it up.
- Always put the shoe on the right foot first.
- Do not speak in the dark.
- When making a sacrifice, go barefoot.

Only a few of Pythagoras' most brilliant pupils, however, after years of patient learning, were allowed to speak or even to ask questions.

Instead, most of his followers had to be satisfied with learning questions and answers such as:

- What are the isles of the blessed?
- The Sun and Moon.
- What is the wisest thing?
- Number.
- What is the Oracle at Delphi?
- The song the sirens sing.

LIFE WITH PYTHAGORAS

If rule number 1 in the Pythagorean 'school' or cult was 'SILENCE!', rule number 2 was that everyone had to be vegetarian. This would not have seemed cultish to the Eastern thinkers and, like the Eastern mystics, Pythagoras believed that human souls were reincarnated in animals.

Pythagoras' followers had to eat meals of honeycomb, millet or barley bread, and vegetables, while the philosopher would pop down to the port and pay fishermen to throw their catch back into the sea. Non-vegetarians think that's a sign of madness, although we can afford to be a bit more charitable with the story of the philosopher telling a ferocious bear to eat barley and acorns, and not to attack humans any more.

Pythagoras not only showed respect for animals, but also for trees, which he insisted were not to be destroyed unless there was absolutely no alternative. On one occasion he even reproved an ox for wantonly trampling corn!

THE HARMONY
OF THE HEAVENS

*When Newton elegantly demonstrated that the mysterious movements of the
cosmos could all be both explained and anticipated by measurements coupled
with mathematics, he acknowledged his debt to Pythagoras.*

In his notes to propositions 4 to 9 of
Principia Mathematica, Newton says
Pythagoras inspired his work:
*'By means of experiments he ascertained
weights by which all tones on equal
strings were reciprocal as the squares of
the lengths of the string… The
proportions discovered… he applied to
the heavens and … by comparing those
weights with those of the planets and the
lengths of the strings with the distances of
the planets he understood by means of*
*the harmony of the heavens that the
weights of the planets towards the Sun
were reciprocally as the squares of their
distances from the Sun.'*

Pythagoras believed that mathematics
offered a glimpse of a perfect reality, of
which our own world is but an imperfect
reflection, and contrasted this pure,
incorruptible, divine realm with the
corruptible, earthly sphere. Sadly, it was
in this sphere that the human soul was
trapped, caught in the body as in a tomb.

*Pythagoras experimented with musical
instruments of various kinds.*

INTRODUCING EUCLID

The message, relayed by Plato, that geometry provided a route towards timeless truths, is epitomised by Euclid's *Elements,* a treatise consisting of 13 separate short texts written in Alexandria around 300 BCE. Euclid proved that all you need are just five assumptions in order to build a pretty darn good geometry.

And these were:

- Things which are equal to the same thing are equal to one another
- If equals are added to equals the wholes are equal
- If equals are subtracted from equals, the remainders are equal
- Things which coincide with one another are equal to one another
- The whole is greater than the part

If you don't like these, then make sure that you steer clear of the proofs! Euclid's approach of setting out his assumptions, then proving something, and then using the 'proved thing' to further develop new proofs, citing only the number of the proof, is incredibly powerful and has ever afterwards proved irresistible to many philosophers.

Statue in honour of Euclid in the Oxford University Museum of Natural History.

HIDDEN ASSUMPTIONS

Euclid considered that his axioms were 'self-evident'. They were statements about physical reality, that anyone could see must be true simply by thinking about them. In fact, they can be faulted for containing hidden assumptions.

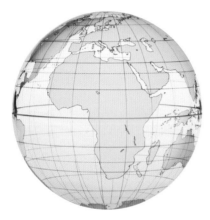

Globe, indicating lines of latitude and longitude.

As an example of a hidden assumption, consider the fifth, so-called 'parallel postulate'. This assumes that parallel lines never meet because it assumes that space is flat, yet parallel lines certainly do meet if you draw them on a sphere.

If you don't believe me, try drawing two parallel lines on a football! At best you will get two 'great circles', like the lines on a globe. Lines of latitude that appear to run parallel to the equator are actually curves. Lines of longitude are parallel when they cross the equator, run straight and meet at the North and South Poles. In mathematical terms, they intersect at two points of a Euclidean segment, or the diameter of the sphere.

Another hidden assumption is that space is homogeneous (the same everywhere) and another is that it is unbounded, both of which are necessary to ensure that any point can be transformed into another point by some mathematical operation, and neither of which are in themselves proven. In fact, the more powerful telescopes get, the less this seems to be true – matter in the universe seems to be distributed unevenly.

Albert Einstein.

NON-EUCLIDEAN EINSTEIN

If the Greeks imagined Euclid's geometry to be the exemplar of pure knowledge, with inviolable rules, Euclidian geometry is nowadays recognised as just one possible kind of geometry. Even Albert Einstein had to be reminded of the fact that there were alternative 'non-Euclidean' universes, before he was able to develop his ground-breaking new physics of relative space-time.

Einstein introduced his radically different new universe at the start of the 20th century. You might say that philosophers should really have figured this out long before, and some philosophers had. Zeno's paradoxes are often treated as amusing curiosities written before that powerful form of maths known as calculus was invented. Such dismissals reflect more on the lack of comprehension of the writers than they do on the issues Zeno raised.

ZENO REVISITED

'In this capricious world, nothing is more capricious than posthumous fame.
One of the most notable victims of posterity's lack of judgement is the Eleatic,
Zeno. Having invented four arguments all immeasurably subtle and profound,
the grossness of subsequent philosophers pronounced him to be a mere
ingenious juggler, and his arguments to be one and all sophisms.
After two thousand years of continual refutation, these sophisms
were reinstated, and made the foundation
of a mathematical renaissance...'

B ertrand Russell certainly did not underrate Zeno's significance when he wrote the above in *The Principles of Mathematics volume I* (1903). And no one disputes the implications of Bertrand Russell's 'Barber Paradox', which he stumbled across in the early years of the 20th century and of which there is more in Chapter 9.

Bertrand Russell, British philosopher,
logician, mathematician, historian,
writer, social critic and political activist.

THE PARADOX

The word 'paradox' comes from the Greek for 'beyond belief'. A paradox is a contradiction, where reasonable assumptions and sound reasoning lead to a ridiculous or otherwise unacceptable conclusion. Zeno's Paradoxes of Motion are an example of this use of the term.

The figure of Euclid forms part of a 14th-century fountain in Nuremberg, Germany.

Another important example in philosophy is the 'Paradox of the Liar', attributed originally to Epimenides. It simply runs 'All Cretans tell lies all the time.' The paradox arises when this claim is made by a Cretan. In such a situation, is the statement true or not?

The point is that the truth of the claim affects the circumstances in which it is uttered, which affects the truth of the claim, which... etc etc. Effectively, the statements are neither true nor false.

Zeno predates Plato, although he may just have known Socrates. He is considerably older than Euclid, whose fabulous geometrical systems, developed from those of the North Africans, so impressed the philosophers and are hardly mentioned by maths teachers. Nonetheless, much of Zeno is about geometry and the nature of numbers – particularly the strange quantities of infinity and zero.

FOUR FROM ZENO

Most of Zeno's paradoxes involve number theory and, just as Zeno challenged the assumptions of his time with his paradoxes of motion, much of the orthodoxy of modern philosophy and mathematics rests on conventions that are certainly not as inevitable as we have become accustomed to thinking.

Lets look at four of Zeno's 40 paradoxes, the four for which he is best remembered.

The Racecourse paradox states that a runner cannot ever reach the finishing line, because first he must get to a point halfway along the course, then a point halfway along the second half of the course, and so on. Because the course can be divided into an infinite number of sections, he must pass through an infinite number of 'half way' points and can, therefore, never reach the end. In fact, he can never actually get started!

In the more famous race between Achilles and the tortoise, (sometimes remembered as a race between a hare and tortoise) Achilles finds that, having given his opponent a head start, he cannot catch up! The reason is that by the time he races to where his opponent was, the tortoise has moved on a little further. He races to that point but, inevitably, the tortoise has advanced a little bit further still.

Start.
2) Half distance.
3) Three- quarters distance.
4) Seven-eighths distance.
5) Fifteen sixteenths.
6) Thirty-one thirty-seconds.
7) Sixty-three sixty-fourths... etc.

In the Arrow paradox, Zeno argues that, if we think of time as a long string of particular instants, or moments, then the arrow must at any given moment have a certain position, and that being at a certain position implies being at rest, so the arrow should fall to the ground.

Lastly, the two rows of moving bodies in the Stadium paradox, offers apparently contradictory conclusions about relative motion. Some philosophers think that Zeno was muddled, but it seems more likely that he was making a subtle point about time and space which history has garbled. (It wouldn't be the first time!)

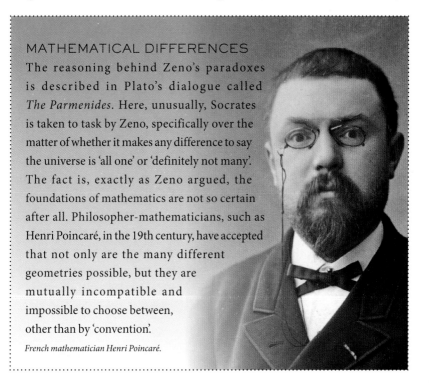

MATHEMATICAL DIFFERENCES

The reasoning behind Zeno's paradoxes is described in Plato's dialogue called *The Parmenides*. Here, unusually, Socrates is taken to task by Zeno, specifically over the matter of whether it makes any difference to say the universe is 'all one' or 'definitely not many'. The fact is, exactly as Zeno argued, the foundations of mathematics are not so certain after all. Philosopher-mathematicians, such as Henri Poincaré, in the 19th century, have accepted that not only are the many different geometries possible, but they are mutually incompatible and impossible to choose between, other than by 'convention'.

French mathematician Henri Poincaré.

THE FIRST MATHEMATICIANS

The rise of Greek philosophy was on the wings of mathematics, so to speak, and mathematics has continued to exert a fascination for philosophers ever since, not least in the efforts of the logicians to reduce human thought to a kind of symbolic notation

There are two main roots to Greek mathematics. The older of the sources is Ancient Egypt, around 3100 to 2500 BCE, and was very sophisticated, as the Pyramids with their mathematical proportions, let alone their positioning with respects to various planetary and solar bodies, testify.

The other source, tapped a thousand years later, is the priests of Mesopotamia, or the 'land between the two rivers', these being the Tigris and the Euphrates. This mathematics was primarily for everyday purposes, for building, for trading and for astronomers to measure the seasons, yet also mystical.

Plato, it turns out, borrowed most of his ideas from mathematically-minded thinkers like Pythagoras and Zeno. What, though, of his pupil, Aristotle? Naturally, Aristotle drew on Plato,

his mentor, for many of his original positions, and that means, as we have seen, also on the Eastern mystics and mathematicians.

In his writings, Aristotle offers some rather disorganised reminiscences of Pythagoras' method, saying that the first thing created is number. He appreciates the logic of it all, that once the universe consists of things distinguished from one another – that is, things that can now be numbered – all kinds of relationships spring into being. Aristotle adds:

… such and such a modification of numbers being justice, and another being soul and reason, another being opportunity – and similarly almost everything being expressible as numbers… they supposed the whole of heaven to be a musical scale and a number…

Aristotle also explains that the Pythagoreans linked numbers to concepts like justice, which is number Four, and marriage, which took the number Five, but the theory is in reality more complicated.

Aristotle towers over many disciplines even now, despite, when you get down to it, having been flat wrong on almost everything he asserted. He's the bloke who insisted that the Earth didn't move but the Sun went round it. He's also the political guru who split humanity into aristocrats and slaves… and women, whom he compares to domestic cattle. Quite possibly a lot of this bad-boy stuff is because Plato's most famous pupil seems to have been determined to disagree with his mentor on all key points. The result, as the 20th century political philosopher Karl Popper puts it, is that Aristotle left philosophy ever afterwards 'in a state of empty verbiage and barren scholasticism.'

Aristotle insisted that the Sun went round the Earth.

Plato and Socrates flank the entrance to the Neoclassical Academy in Athens, Greece.

Aristotle is rightly considered one of the great figures of philosophy and natural science, particularly for putting logic at the centre of philosophy.

He marks the watershed in Greek philosophy, born 15 years after the execution of Socrates in 399 BCE, and studied at the Academy in Athens under Plato until 347 BCE.

He had hoped to be Plato's successor, but his approach was out of favour with the mathematicians of the time, so Plato's nephew, Speussippus, took over instead.

Aristotle's greatest achievement is supposed to have been his 'Laws of Thought', part of his attempt to put everyday language on a logical footing. His *Prior Analytics* is the first attempt to create a system of formal deductive logic, while the *Posterior Analytics* attempts to use this to systematise scientific knowledge. Like many contemporary philosophers, he regarded logic as providing the key to philosophical progress. The traditional 'Laws of Thought' are that:

- Whatever is, is (the law of identity);
- Nothing can both be and not be (the law of non-contradiction); and
- Everything must either be or not be (the law of excluded middle).

Put another way, the laws are saying:

- All apples are apples.
- If something is not an apple, then, well it cannot be considered to be an apple. And (finally)
- Something can't both be an apple and be 'not an apple' at the same time.

Well, it looks like stating the obvious but, in fact, and in spite of how dominant these laws of thought have been, they have not been without their critics, and philosophers from Heraclitus to Hegel have levelled powerful arguments against them.

It is Parmenides, (one of the Pre-Socratic philosophers in the 5th century BCE) who is credited with originally setting out the second rule, the law of non-contradiction, put also as 'Never will this prevail, that what is not is,' by Plato in *The Sophist*.

TROUBLE WITH THE LAWS

If it seems strange that the principle of non-contradiction needed inventing, it should be explained that before Parmenides the natural way of thinking was that everything was a bit of both.

The inflexible logic of the 'Laws of Thought' imposed a new kind of world under a new kind of authority.

Before, the commonsense assumption was, as Heraclitus says:

Immanuel Kant challenged the basis of the 'Laws of Thought'.

'Cold things grow warm; warm grows cold; wet grows dry; parched grows moist.'

By 1763, Aristotle's logical laws were causing philosophers problems, prompting Immanuel Kant to publish 'An attempt to introduce the concept of negative quantities into science.' This treatise sought to identify internal contradictions in abstract metaphysical theories derived from pure logic. Kant pointed out that, in reality, something can be both A and not A – both an apple and no an apple.

Consider, for instance, that a body can be both in motion and not-in-motion, since it depends on the perspective of who is looking. Cups of coffee on trains offer a good example of this. If you are sitting on the train the cup of coffee is (fortunately) 'not in motion'. But to someone watching the train whizz past, it certainly is!

Georg Wilhelm Friedrich Hegel.

HEGEL'S TRUE REALITY

In the 19th century, despite being very much in favour of strong rulers, the political philosopher, Georg W. Hegel, decided it was actually better for philosophy to return to Heraclitus' position that change, and in particular contradiction and conflict, is the 'true reality', and the static unchanging world of the 'Laws of Thought' is a false, misleading one. Add to which, Hegel says, the law of identity says very little in itself. The fact that A = A is no more than a tautology and has little meaning. It tells us almost nothing about the identity of a thing.

The only way a thing truly takes on identity is through its otherness, or what it is not. Pythagoras could scarcely have put it better.

CHAPTER 3
SEEKING WISDOM
THROUGH GOD

'How is it they live in such harmony the billions of stars – when most men can barely go a minute without declaring war in their minds about someone they know.'

Thomas Aquinas, 13th Century

THE 'VIRTUOUS WAR'

Philosophy and theology are often two opposing factions. Browsing the introductory philosophy texts in a bookshop, you find tirades like The God Delusion *and* Against Bull**** (bull**** *being quintessentially faith-based beliefs) penned by those who see philosophy as engaged in a kind of virtuous war against irrationalism.*

In some universities where I have worked, even though the departments were usually physically located alongside, the philosophy and theology lecturers operated a code of silence with each other, while each bitterly reproving each others' errors, both in private and in public.

Bertrand Russell once said of philosophy that it is stranded in 'the no-man's land between science and theology, exposed to attacks from both sides', but today it is more theology that is in the middle and wilting under fire. For a thousand years, however, from the time of Augustine up to the Renaissance,

Modern philosophy and theology lecturers do not always see eye to eye.

the situation was very different. Then, the greatest minds were solely concerned with building up and perfecting the Christian doctrines which were seen as being the very highest and purest philosophy.

With very few exceptions, all the thinkers who contributed significantly to the intellectual life were churchmen.

'Until the 14th century, ecclesiastics have a virtual monopoly of philosophy, and philosophy, accordingly, is written from the standpoint of the church.'

Bertrand Russell,
History of Western Philosophy, 1946.

Most of these thinkers operated within the Christian church, at the time the key social institution, its monasteries guarding the great texts and acting very like research universities. The church was also a social and political force, exercising at this time far greater control over the lives of the ordinary people than any regional, far less national, institutions.

Philosophy and theology in conflict – 6th-century Greek philosopher and mathematician Pythagoras (left) and 14th-century English theologian and church reformer John Wycliffe.

The Middle Ages was a time of the collapse for many national (and regional) governments following the waves of invaders – be they the Vikings from the North, the 'Barbarians' from the East, or the Moors from the south – that swept over the once proud cities of Europe.

It was through religious scholars that the story of philosophy continued at this time, with the ideas of the ancient philosophers, notably of Plato and Aristotle, consulted in exactly the same reverential way as the holy texts of the Torah, Bible and Koran.

The first half of the period was the turn of Plato, championed by Augustine; in the second half, Aristotle increasingly came to the fore, championed by Thomas Aquinas. We'll hear a lot more about

Marauders such as the Vikings brought havoc to Europe in the Middle Ages.

both of these two in a moment, but first let's recall the context.

The great flowering of European culture epitomised by the School of Athens had been spread far and wide by the Romans, whose empire, at its height, stretched from Britain and the Atlantic in the north to North Africa and the Middle East (or Mesopotamia as it was called then).

But on 24 August 410, the good times came to an end. It was on this date that the barbarians entered Rome.

The sack of the city sent a thrill of horror round the Roman world: 'In one city,' St Jerome wrote, 'the whole world perished.' By the end of the 5th century the western Roman Empire was no more, and Europe had entered the Dark Ages.

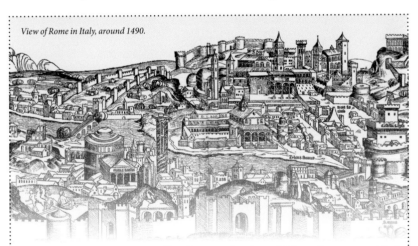

View of Rome in Italy, around 1490.

Of course, reality was actually a bit more complicated than that – but for a thousand years it is true that philosophy retreated from the towns and cities, which no longer provided a safe base, and developed instead under the protection, and guidance, of organised religion.

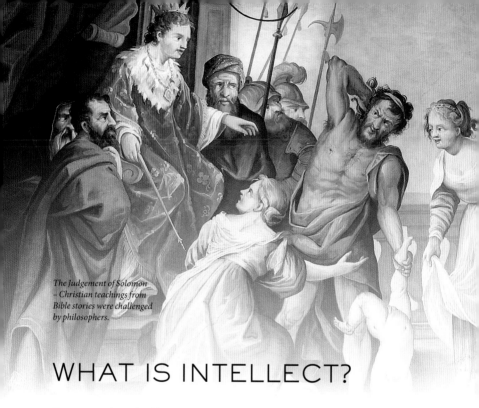

The Judgement of Solomon – Christian teachings from Bible stories were challenged by philosophers.

WHAT IS INTELLECT?

Europe owed much of her knowledge during the Middle Ages to Arabian writers in general and Islamic theologians in particular. Scholars such as Averroes and Maimonides (a Sephardic Jew living in Arab territory) were especially important.

Even where the Islamic philosophers, were not particularly original, they were key links in the chain of ideas that led from the Ancient world to the modern.

Averroes' enthusiasm for the writings of Aristotle contributed greatly to Aristotle's status for many years not merely as 'The Philosopher' but as a prophet. Aristotle's view was that the soul is not immortal at all, but only the intellect, called nous, is.

AVERROES AND ALLEGORY

The most interesting thing about Averroes is his argument that religious truth is not literal but allegorical. The vexed issue of the origins of life and evolution, still the cause of so much controversy, he briskly solves by saying that the religious tales are metaphorical, not literal, and the scientific accounts are perfectly possible to adopt.

Averroes thus leaves a humanist legacy by abolishing the immortal soul, and by putting science ahead of religious teachings. But that said, he does not see himself really as offering new ideas, but rather as accurately transmitting the ideas of the Ancients to a new world. Averroes also says that concepts like the idea of creation out of nothing are impossible for ordinary people to grasp, and so the religious texts offer allegories and metaphors to make their points. The idea that there is no individual soul coexistent with each individual's body is likewise there in the texts but hidden by the use of metaphorical language.

Averroes believed that the religious stories of the Creation were metaphorical, not literal.

This perspective caused problems for the later Christian philosophers. What did Aristotle mean by the intellect – was it maybe something like the personality? Unlikely, because, as Averroes warns, the idea seems to be that intellect is not the property of individuals but rather transcends them. This view, of course, undercut the Christian teachings about individual responsibility and chances of redemption and was considered deeply heretical.

Since Averroes was more faithful to Aristotle than to the texts, notably those making up the Koran, he was in later life accused of heresy and many of his books were burnt.

Ironically, his influence was greater on Christian than on Islamic philosophy.

The Christian monasteries that were the European repositories not only of the written texts, but the philosophical debates too, reconnected with the Ancient world via the Islamic scholars and their careful translations of the lost classics.

It would not be until the growth of trade, bringing with it new dynamism and sophistication to the trading centres, that a rival body of intellectuals would emerge with different perspectives.

Economically, the Middles Ages – the Dark Ages – saw the great majority of people living at a reduced level in which life was physically a struggle, and poverty and disease were everywhere. In such conditions, it made sense that most people concentrated on survival and entrusted philosophy to the priests

Averroes was accused of heresy and his books burned.

and monks. These in turn promised the people that if their everyday lives were hard, through virtue (through following the injunctions of the church and paying their alms) happiness would surely be theirs – in the ever after.

The power of the church was increased by the importance of its role as a provider of charity. The desperate and destitute could easily be encouraged to behave as a mob, whipped into a frenzy for particular tasks by a sermon or two, just one example being the cruel murder of Alexandria's brilliant woman mathematician and philosopher, Hypatia. As for the Pope, he remained 'merely' the Bishop of Rome and not a significant force elsewhere, throughout the Middle Ages.

Death of the philosopher Hypatia, in Alexandria.

Notre Dame in Paris – it was around abbeys and the great cathedrals that modern universities developed.

ANCIENT AND MODERN

While religious centres became seats of modern learning, the religious doctrine of life as a sacrifice for heavenly rewards, which has been so historically influential (Marx condemned it as the 'opiate of the masses', stopping people from demanding a better life is a development of the ancient Greek philosophers' teaching that the sensible world (meaning the physical world accessible to the senses), which exists in space and time, is just and illusion.

Plato urged the elite to live not in this world but to transcend it to the world of ideas, notably those of truth and love and beauty. What the Islamic and Christian churches did was to take this Greek approach and make the eternal world available only after death! It's a small change but one, as they say, of the utmost importance.

If, in recent years, 'radical Islam' has created a different image of the

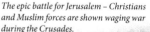

Islam was far more civilised than Christianity in the Middle Ages.

scapegoats for all kinds of social ills, while the Islamic countries offered Jews considerable respect and autonomy. This is why, even today, Iran, an Islamic state, contains the largest Diaspora of Jews outside Israel.

The Christians were pretty vicious to each other, too. Different sects argued over the true nature of Christianity. One, called the Gnostics, refused to allow that the Son of God could ever

religion, during this thousand year period, Islam was very much more civilised and humane than Christianity. Christians regularly slaughtered Jews, who were used as convenient

have been a squalling baby, far less be executed, and insisted that Jesus was merely a prophet speaking on behalf of God. This view influenced Mohammed and became a key tenet of Islam.

The epic battle for Jerusalem – Christians and Muslim forces are shown waging war during the Crusades.

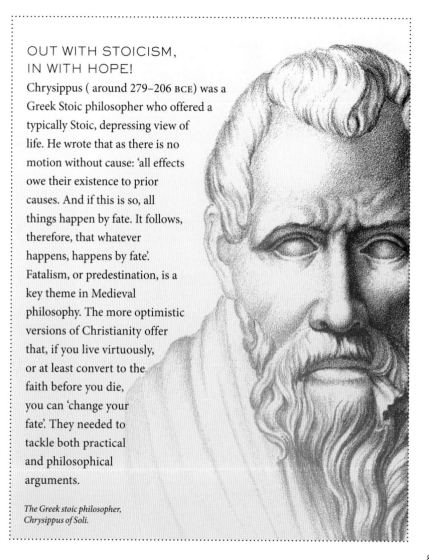

OUT WITH STOICISM, IN WITH HOPE!

Chrysippus (around 279–206 BCE) was a Greek Stoic philosopher who offered a typically Stoic, depressing view of life. He wrote that as there is no motion without cause: 'all effects owe their existence to prior causes. And if this is so, all things happen by fate. It follows, therefore, that whatever happens, happens by fate'. Fatalism, or predestination, is a key theme in Medieval philosophy. The more optimistic versions of Christianity offer that, if you live virtuously, or at least convert to the faith before you die, you can 'change your fate'. They needed to tackle both practical and philosophical arguments.

The Greek stoic philosopher, Chrysippus of Soli.

FIRST THERE WAS THE WORD

The followers of Origen, the early Christian theologian, who lived in the late second and early third century CE, *took Plato's view that souls are separate from people, extending it to the point where things like stars have souls, too.*

Eventually, Origen thought, all the souls will become reunited, even those that had at some time or another been trapped in the body of human wrongdoers. All this was highly heretical.

Origen believed that souls could become trapped in human bodies.

Origen made another error that was both theological and practical – he became a eunuch as a way of escaping the vile 'temptations of the flesh', citing a New Testament text that reads:

> *'There be eunuchs which have made themselves eunuchs for the kingdom of heaven's sake.'*

One of the great religious thinkers of the Middle Ages was an Irish man confusingly called John the Scot, who lived most of the time… in France. John's greatest work, called *On Nature*, splits the universe into four categories of things.

- That which creates but is not created
- That which creates and is created
- That which is created but does not create

And finally:

- That which is neither created nor creates other things.

SEEKING WISDOM THROUGH GOD

Bishop George Berkeley.

There is only one thing in the first category – God. The interesting division is actually between the second and third categories. The second is really the Platonic realm of ideas or 'forms', and the third is the humdrum world of 'things' that exist in space and time and which can be perceived. What then of the fourth category? It is God again.

It may look odd, but reasoning thus serves to 'close the cycle'. The Platonic world of ideas is thus created, in the way that the book of Genesis in the Bible describes: first there was the Word – or Logos, as it is often put, using the Latin term.

Logos, by making possible ideas, creates the divisions in the flux of physical reality. If we did not have the concept of (say) tree, we would not have any trees. It is this view that another great Irish philosopher, Bishop Berkeley promoted in the early 18th century, and the issue has still not gone away.

John the Scot did not see men and women as being morally equal, women being the major sinners.

Another influential idea of John the Scot is that sin created the division of humanity into two halves – not good and evil but male and female.

Women are the sinners, forever tempting men into bad ways. But don't be too harsh on John – this view, comfortable enough for male writers and their male readers, can be seen anyway in many ancient texts (Plato being the exception).

Speaking of misogynist views brings us nicely to those iconic figures of Catholic philosophy, Augustine and Aquinas. Saint Augustine's (whose life marks the very start of the medieval period) writings on metaphysics, ethics (the quite racy *Confessions*!), and politics (the classic book *The City of God*) remain important today. Influential ideas include his metaphysical analysis of time, his analysis of evil, and his view of the conditions for justified war.

His most direct impact comes from his role in systematising Christian teachings and making them indeed more 'logical'.

The certainty of the existence of the will as a solution to the problem of evil, not to mention as the precursor to Descartes principle: 'I think therefore I am', is found in Book VII of the *Confessions*, where Augustine writes:

> *'I knew myself to have a will in the same way and as much as I knew myself to be alive. Therefore when I willed or did not will something, I was utterly certain that none other than myself was willing or not willing.'*

Recognising that he had control of his own free will means that Augustine is the true author of Descartes' and modern philosophy's great principle 'I think therefore I am'.

The Benedictine monk, Thomas Anselm, also followed in Augustine's footsteps, producing one of the classic arguments for believing in God, the so- called Ontological proof.

Augustine was born and died in North Africa, which was then part of the Roman Empire. He taught philosophy in Rome and Milan, converted to Christianity in 387 and was consecrated the Bishop of Hippo in 395.

St. Augustine wrote of babies as though they were evil.

roads and potholes. In fact, all difficult ideas fell within the domain of the religious authorities, and this seemed only natural, indeed sensible, as only the churchmen were really educated or cultured enough to command respect for their decisions.

In his other main work, the celebrated autobiographical *Confessions*, Augustine starts by discussing his evil nature and describes how in his 16th year, while away from school ('a season of idleness being interposed through the narrowness of my parents' fortunes'), the 'briers of unclean desires grew rank over my head, and there was no hand to root them out.' And, as one recent commentator writes disapprovingly: 'At the age of 16, he failed to contain his lust and sinned. The name of the woman involved is not known.' The 'sin' produced a little boy. Augustine seems to have loved his child despite evidently not being a fan of babies. These, he insists, are evil creatures.

In the *City of God*, Augustine splits social life into two parts, with the Church responsible for the codes and morals and the secular state responsible for the

'He could not yet speak and, pale with jealousy and bitterness, glared at his brother sharing his mother's milk... it can hardly be innocence, when the source of milk is flowing richly and abundantly, not to endure a share going to one's blood brother, who is in profound need, dependent for life exclusively on that one food.'

Saint Augustine, *Confessions*, Book I VII

Noah condemned his grandson, Canaan, into slavery after feeling Canaan had humiliated him.

THE ESCAPE CLAUSE

Fortunately, there is a way out. For Augustine righteousness comes by dying. Joy!
'It was then said to man, "You will die if you sin." Now it is said to the martyrs,
"Die, rather than sin."'

Years later, in his thirties, Augustine offers his famous prayer *da mihi castitatem et continentiam, sed noli modo comes*. 'Grant me chastity and continence – but not yet.' It was soon after, however, that he is supposed to have received a divine revelation that made him resolve henceforth to devote his life to the church.

Saint Augustine's particular kind of morality made him a strong advocate of slavery, which (long before the British invented the actual slave trade) was a widespread feature of the medieval world, taking on many different forms.

Augustine traced the practice back to 'righteous' Noah who 'branded the sin of his son' with that name, and established the principle that the good were entitled to use the sinful. He explains in *The City of God*, 'The prime cause, then, of slavery is sin, which brings man under the dominion of his fellow – that which does not happen save by the judgment of God, with whom is no unrighteousness, and who knows how to award fit punishments to every variety of offence.'

During the Flood, all but a handful of humankind were swept away as sinners.

But how did Augustine know all this? It is not in the Bible, after all. Indeed, the Bible never mentions 'Original Sin' as such, and Augustine's ideas are in direct contradiction to some passages, such as that at Ezekiel 18, where it is stated that only the sinner will die and their children are innocent.

Of course, Augustine's authority is God Himself. Augustine considered 'revelations' he received to be true, even if apparently in direct contradiction of the Bible. 'Divine revelation, not reason, is the source of all truth.' Like Bishop Origen before him, Augustine interpreted Scripture allegorically. The Bible, he believed, had been veiled by God to weed out the worthy from the unworthy amongst those seeking Him.

A Latin Bible.

Even at the time, some Christian intellectuals complained that Augustine made it seem as if the devil were the maker of humanity. They found it absurd to claim that newborn infants were cursed, and they believed that

The three wise monkeys – See, Hear and Speak No Evil. Pelagius said we had more choice.

this contradicted God's love of justice. A Welsh monk called Morgan, but known as Pelagius, counter-argued that, as sin was something of the soul and not the body, it could not be transmitted from generation to generation.

Rather than being born sinful, people could make choices between good and evil, he insisted, and were indeed responsible for their choices. Pelagius also criticised Augustine for being biased towards the wealthy by offering them the prospect of God's favour as long as they left their land to Catholic monasteries when they died.

This last was too much for both Augustine and the Pope, who decided to 'excommunicate' Pelagius. The monk was obliged to return to Britain and stay there for the rest of his life. Woe indeed!

The other great figure from the thousand years of Catholic philosophy is undoubtedly Thomas Aquinas (1225–1274). All of his life Aquinas was very overweight, suffered from oedema (dropsy), and had one large eye and one small eye, making him look lop-sided. He was always introspective and frequently silent. When he did speak, it was often unrelated to the conversation.

He decided to become a monk and he made a very good one, canonised (proclaimed a saint) by Pope John XXII in 1323 and, 200 or so years later, recognised as a 'doctor of the church', henceforth to be known as the 'Angelic Doctor'. This honour was principally for his years spent toiling over the *Summa Theologiae*, or *'Summary of Theology'*.

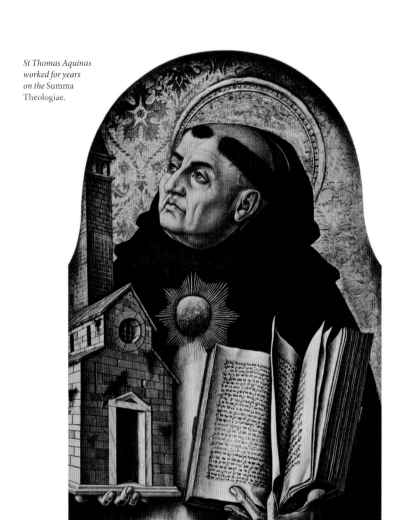

St Thomas Aquinas worked for years on the Summa Theologiae.

QUESTIONS, QUESTIONS

Because of the diverse conditions of humans, it happens that some acts are virtuous to some people, as appropriate and suitable to them, while the same acts are immoral for others, as inappropriate to them.

Thomas Aquinas

The *Summa* consisted of 518 questions and 2,652 responses. Work on it took seven years from 1266 through 1273. It is written in the style of the times in the form of 'challenges'. Medieval people, and not just their philosophers, loved these verbal

Medieval philosophers debated the existence of God.

sparring sessions, known as *obligationes*, during which opponents were obliged to either assent, dissent or doubt statements.

The first person to end up contradicting themselves lost. The first dispute in the *Summa Theologiae* is over the nature of theology and the second is over God's existence. In fact, the concerns of medieval philosophy are frequently binary: good versus evil; time versus timeless eternity; the nature of matter and life versus the nature of the soul and of God.

Philosophers, not to mention the Church, have usually emphasised Aquinas's arguments for the existence of God, rather than his excellent arguments against. These are much more original and interesting. For example, in Article 3 of the *Summa Theologiae*, headed 'Whether God exists', Aquinas notes (philosophically) that it seems that God does not exist, for if one of two contrary things were infinite, its opposite would be completely destroyed. Since by 'God,' we mean some infinite good, it follows that, if God existed, evil would not. However, evil does exist in the world. Therefore God does not exist.

That's essentially the argument about evil in a nutshell. A second argument evokes what is sometimes called the principle of parsimony and associated with William of Ockham (c. 1287–1347). This is that 'one should not needlessly multiply elements in an explanation'. All natural effects can be traced to natural causes, and all contrived effects can be traced to human will. Thus there is no need to suppose that God exists.

Aquinas's own rebuttal of his sceptical arguments seems very half-hearted. As to the first point, he recalls merely that Saint Augustine wrote that 'since God is the supreme good he would permit no evil in his works unless he were so omnipotent and good that he could produce good even out of evil'. Aquinas may not say so, but it is all too clear that an all-good, all-powerful God could also make good out of good. Why bring in evil?

If God does not exist, then what of Heaven and Hell?

Medieval philosophers and theologians attempted to find reasons to justify war.

However, Aquinas's discussion of the second argument against God's existence is more detailed. 'It must be said that God's existence can be proved in five ways,' he says. He doesn't go into the five ways, though, because he maintains that it has well been observed that if one argument works, you don't need a second, and if you do produce one, it tends to undermine the first.

Perhaps that is why Martin Luther called the *Summa Theologica* 'the fountain and original soup of all heresy, error, and Gospel havoc', and in 1277 the archbishop of Paris even tried to have Thomas formally condemned!

Philosophers as well as theologians still rate Aquinas very highly for many of his arguments. One such is his definition of 'Just wars'. This starts by saying that a war is just when it is started and controlled by the authority of state or ruler, and then says, 'There must be a just cause', and that, 'The war must be for good, or against evil.'

Perhaps sensing a weakness in the Angelic Doctor's work here, for it seems to have an element of the tautological about it by involving elements of justice in deciding which wars are 'just', or perhaps concerned that the approach opens the way to rather a lot of wars,

Until the Middle Ages, most philosophers considered slaves to have no rights whatsoever.

two more rules were later added by the Catholic Church. These were that the war must be a last resort and that the methods used must be proportionate to the injustice. Like Augustine, Aquinas also looked at the question of the rights of slaves and, by extension, feudal serfs. Most philosophers (following Aristotle) considered slaves to have no rights whatsoever. Aquinas basically agreed,

asserting that some men belonged to others, just as sons belonged to their fathers. He adds, 'men of outstanding intelligence naturally take command, while those who are less intelligent but of more robust physique, seem intended by nature to act as servants.'

Proof comes from the Biblical descriptions of heaven, where some angels were superior to others.

Thomas Aquinas stated that not all Christians, no matter how pious they might seem, were guaranteed a place in heaven.

On the issue of money lending, however, he ruled (again following Aristotle) that this practice was unnatural, and so forbidden. Aquinas actually thinks that business in general, has a certain '*inhonestas*' about it. '*Inhonestas*' does not exactly mean dishonesty, it means 'something unworthy,' or perhaps, 'something not quite fitting.'

The problem with all the exchanges is that one party tries to get a little bit more out of the exchange than they put in. That's *inhonestas*! In the medieval social pyramid, with aristocrats and bishops at the top – tradespeople came right at the bottom, certainly lower than those who worked the land.

Aquinas also ruled on many minor issues. He left evidence of a surprisingly active letter-writing career, responding to queries often from complete strangers, even rather ridiculous questions. When somebody, for instance, asked him whether the names of all the blessed were written on a scroll exhibited in heaven, he wrote back, 'So far as I can see, this

is not the case; but there is no harm in saying so.' Sorrow, he advises, 'can be alleviated by good sleep, a bath and a glass of wine'.

On the great question of whether a good Christian was sure to avoid eternal damnation, Aquinas was less reassuring. He notes that in the time of Noah, the entire human race was submerged by the Deluge, bar the lucky eight saved in the Ark. He recalls that Saint Augustine had written: 'And these eight people who were saved signify that very few Christians are saved, because there are very few who sincerely renounce the world, and those who renounce it only in words do not belong to the mystery represented by that ark.'

So Thomas himself concludes that the great majority of Catholics (let alone anyone else) are damned. Aquinas explains, regretfully, 'Because eternal beatitude surpasses the natural state, especially since it has been deprived of original grace, it is the little number that are saved.'

SAINTS PRESERVED

But could a virtuous saint really bear to see so many others eternally damned? You betcha! Thomas even offers that this will be a perk of being one of the saved!

Thomas wrote: 'That the saints may enjoy their beatitude and the grace of God more abundantly, they are permitted to see the punishment of the damned in hell.'

If Aquinas's medieval warnings look bizarre and dated today (and I hope they do), his method remains impressive, a return to the style of Socrates and the open philosophical examination of great issues. Arguments, Aquinas insists, should be based not 'on documents of faith, but on the reasons and statements of the philosophers themselves.'

This was a major advance and contributed to the next stage in the story of philosophy.

Aquinas said that saints could witness the suffering of the damned.

Portrait of Saint Thomas Aquinas at the University of Cusco, Peru.

As one of St Thomas' final acts, he was called upon by the Church authorities to defend the status of religious knowledge against Siger of Brabant's claim that something could be true in theology even if demonstrably false in science and philosophy.

Aquinas believed that religious and scientific or philosophical truths, far from being contradictory, were different sides of the same truth; indeed, they complement each other. He was determined to win that argument, and help prevent the Church becoming irrelevant in matters of knowledge.

After the debate, his followers hailed what they saw as a most convincing victory. Yet, instead of being encouraged, Aquinas simply stopped writing altogether.

The story goes that, while saying mass on December 6, 1273, he experienced a heavenly vision and, when urged to take up his pen again, he replied, 'Such things have been revealed to me that all that I have written seems to me as so much straw. Now I await the end of my days.' And although still not quite 50 years old, he died just three months later. Spooky!

CHAPTER 4
THE RENAISSANCE AND
THE TRIUMPH OF REASON

'Whoever in discussion adduces authority uses not intellect but rather memory...'

Leonardo da Vinci

Leonardo da Vinci, the most celebrated artist of all time.

WHAT IF?

If the historical period rather pointedly named the Dark Ages is all about thinking guided by tradition and religious texts, the Renaissance is all about thinking that has been set free to roam wherever curiosity leads.

With the new approach comes an unparalleled time of artistic creativity and scientific discovery. At least, that is the conventional view. Naturally, the truth is a little more nuanced than that. What seems to have really been going on was much more of a smooth progression and shift that took centuries, propelled in large part by economic forces.

French philosopher Rene Descartes in an engraving from the 1850s.

One such economic bellwether is that by the 12th century, cities had begun to make their presence felt again in Europe, and along with them came new opportunities for sharing ideas, research and learning. Rapidly growing trading settlements such as Venice, Paris, Bruges and London were each home to more than 10,000 people.

This was the golden age of Italy and the backdrop to Machiavelli writing his classic guide for rulers – *The Prince*; of Leonardo da Vinci making a number of important discoveries and painting the 'Mona Lisa', and of Michelangelo painting the Sistine Chapel. The end of the period has Galileo discovering the key principles of relativity – as well as becoming embroiled in that famous dispute with the Church over whether or not the Sun goes round the Earth, or vice versa.

A wealthy international trade centre, Venice also became important in the development of Renaissance culture.

The shift away from the examination of holy texts also sees a new willingness to pose hypothetical questions. This is the era to ask 'what if?' The Renaissance produced a rich crop of thought experiments, including those of Galileo, Descartes, Newton and Leibniz. Descartes used the technique particularly enthusiastically, offering in his Meditations (1641) the original 'brain in a vat' scenario, along with a 'possible world' peopled by automata, another run by a 'malicious Demon.'

MIND GAMES

'All truths are easy to understand once they are discovered; the point is to discover them.'

Galileo Galilei

Perhaps the most influential thought experimenter of them all was Galileo. The Italian philosopher and mathematician did not actually drop two balls, a large one and a small one, off the top of the Leaning Tower of Pisa. Rather, it was a thought experiment, and

The Leaning Tower in Pisa, Italy, featured in Galileo's thought experiment.

it proved, through logic, that all bodies must fall at the same rate – ignoring air resistance, of course. Centuries later, in a slightly garbled tribute to him, the Apollo astronauts would drop a feather and a hammer in the vacuum of the Moon.

Another powerful argument of Galileo's asks us to imagine we are on a ship in a cabin observing goldfish that swim towards the front of their bowl and butterflies that continue their flight around the cabin entirely indifferent to the ship's motion. This simple analogy not only provided the foundations of relativity, but ushered in a world in which dogmatic assertion began to weaken.

Take the relationship between Tycho Brahe, the most famous astronomer of the 16th century (who lost his nose in a duel and always after had to wear a false one), and the King of Denmark. Tycho was a heavy drinker and frequently fell out with his employer. It was in a rage that he took his instruments off to Germany and it was only there, after his death, that

his assistant, Johann Kepler finished the map of the heavens. It was almost by chance that, in order to complete his new, mathematical model of the universe, Kepler resurrected some small parts of Copernicus' earlier work. Notably, the bit where the Earth is set in motion around the Sun.

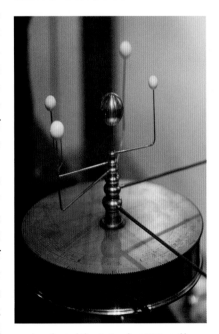

A mechanical planetarium from 1766, used by John Winthrop to teach astronomy at Harvard.

Statue of Tycho Brahe in front of the observatory at Rosenborg Castle in Copenhagen, Denmark.

How much of a scientific revolution is that? Rather less than it might seem. The short and sweet version is that Copernicus 'discovered' that the Earth revolves around the Sun.

Whereas, actually, the idea is an old one, much debated by the Ancients, appearing in influential Sanskrit, Arabian and Roman texts, and well rehearsed by the ancient Greeks. Some of the accounts were pretty detailed too.

In one ancient text, called *The Sand Reckoner* (the name reflecting one of the tasks undertaken: to determine an upper bound for the number of grains of sand that could be fitted into the universe), the celebrated inventor and mathematician, Archimedes, records enthusiastically that someone else called 'Aristarchus' had just brought out a book on the workings of the heavens including exciting hypotheses such as:

- the stars and the Sun remain unmoved, while the Earth turns on its axis.
- the Earth revolves about the Sun in the circumference of a circle, with the Sun lying in the middle of the orbit.
- the distance to the sphere of the fixed stars, starting with the Sun at the centre point, is absolutely enormous.

THE DARK ARTS OF THE NEW AGE

During the Renaissance, Astrology was a fundamental tool for making sense of nature. Tycho Brahe's introduced the course of lectures he gave in Copenhagen in 1574 by stressing the importance of astrology on the grounds of correspondences between the heavenly bodies, terrestrial substances (metals, stones etc.), and bodily organs.

Similarly, Tycho's interest in alchemy, particularly the medical alchemy associated with Paracelsus, was almost as long-standing as his study of astronomy, and his astronomical observatory at Uraniborg was constructed to have two functions: both as an observatory and a alchemical laboratory.

Tycho stressed the importance of studying alchemy and astrology together by having a pair of emblems created. These bore the Latin mottoes: 'By looking down I see upward' and 'By looking up I see downward.'

Equiangulator of Tycho Brahe.

WANDERING PLANETS

Archimedes notes that the new book was influential enough that Cleanthes , the head of the Greek Stoic movement, thought it worth advocating the prosecution of Aristarchus on charges of impiety. Galileo and the Pope were but the repeat show!

Aristarchus was specifically accused of: 'putting in motion the hearth of the universe... [and] supposing the heaven to remain at rest and the Earth to revolve in an oblique circle, while it rotates, at the same time, about its own axis...'

However, Aristarchus was never prosecuted, even if his 'book' seemed to disappear. Only the more muddled theory of the Pythagoreans in which both the Earth and the Sun orbit another 'central fire' was left to challenge the everyday impression that we actually do live on a stationary rock while the heavens and Sun whirl around us.

Then, many centuries later, along came a book, *De Revolutinibus Orbium Coelestrium* or, as it is usually translated, *On the Revolutions of the Heavenly Spheres*. It had been written

Archimedes was excited by Aristarchus' new book.

by Copernicus, a modest Polish priest and part-time astronomer with an essentially theological desire to bring the heavenly 'wanderers' back into the fold. Copernicus did this by firmly placing all the wanderers into circular orbits. In fact, it was only incidentally, as the price of this system tidying, that the Earth itself was set into motion, making it just another planet orbiting an immobile Sun.

It's often forgotten that Copernicus was actually a churchman. Yet it makes sense that he would be, as, actually, whatever the popular perception, throughout the Dark Ages the Church had been an enthusiastic supporter of the new astronomy. That is why, far from seeing himself as a 'revolutionary', least of all a theological one, Copernicus saw himself to be an obedient and diligent Catholic (and one who took mathematical innovations, without attribution, from the Islamic astronomers). He even dedicated his book to Pope Paul III, who received it 'cordially'.

Statue of Polish priest Nicolaus Copernicus in Warsaw, Poland.

The 'Copernican Revolution' we hear so much about today, in terms of scientists overthrowing established orthodoxies, seems to have been conjured up, or perhaps merely misunderstood, by historians.

As one philosopher of science, Bernard Cohen, puts it: literally, the revolution 'was not at all Copernican, but was at best Galilean and Keplerian.' But that does not have quite the same ring to it.

The Church authorities in Copernicus' time were quite prepared to countenance additional refinements of Ptolemy's (regularly updated) model of the universe. The drama came not so much with the Catholics but from the Protestant 'fundamentalists' who objected to all such mathematical explorations – and that battle for 'real Christianity' was yet still just brewing.

Italian physicist, astronomer, mathematician and philosopher Galileo Galilei argued in favour of Copernicus.

Copernicus' idea was not so controversial at the point when Galileo dusted it off and decided to argue forcefully for Copernicus.

Galileo was not a great diplomat. In his acerbically witty *Dialogue on Two Great World Systems* (1632), he not only made it clear that he considered the defenders of Aristotle and Ptolemy, from the Pope to the Professors, to be intellectual clowns, but could not resist ridiculing fellow Copernicans, too.

Most of all, Galileo made a clown out of Simplicio, one of the main characters of the dialogue, whose role was to be a silly mouthpiece for the new Pope's, Urban V's, views on the workings of the Solar System. These were actually pragmatic – the Pope had various factions within his own Church to placate. As late as April 1615, Cardinal Robert Bellarmine, as 'Master of Controversial Questions' at the Inquisition, wrote a letter stating that it was perfectly acceptable to maintain Copernicanism as a working hypothesis; and if there were 'real proof' that the Earth circles around the sun, 'then we should have to proceed with great circumspection in explaining passages of Scripture which appear to teach the contrary...'

Devices such as this armillary sphere were used to chart the stars and planets.

Mind you, the same Cardinal had some years earlier arranged for another Copernican to be burnt at the stake in Rome.

Poor Giordano Bruno was tortured for years by the 'Holy Office' and charged with 'Holding opinions contrary to the Catholic faith', with these opinions pertaining to Jesus as Christ; the virginity of the Virgin Mary; the Trinity, divinity of Christ and Incarnation; Transubstantiation and Mass, and a wealth of other misdeeds.

Eventually, Bruno, a Dominican monk, as well as being a philosopher, a poet, an astronomer and a mathematician was delivered, naked and bound, to the Civil Authorities in Rome with a note stating that he was an incorrigible heretic, but that they should be merciful in their punishment.

'Merciful' though, in the Church's view at this time, meant burning him at the stake.

This sad end to one of Europe's most original philosophical thinkers is often linked directly to the astronomical debate, but in truth it seems much more likely to have had something to do with the fact that Bruno was a rebel monk who had wrote many books, and it was in his writing that he denied the divinity of Jesus. He also went so far as to argue that even the Devil would never face God's judgement.

Those theoretical differences over the ordering of the Solar System scarcely rated in comparison.

Bronze statue of Giordano Bruno at Campo de' Fiori in Rome, Italy.

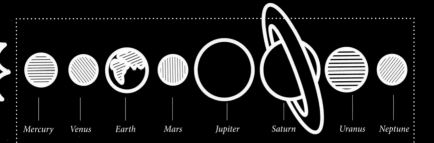

Mercury Venus Earth Mars Jupiter Saturn Uranus Neptune

NEW TECHNOLOGIES, CHANGED PERSPECTIVES

When Galileo heard about the invention of 'spyglasses' in Holland, he built a telescope of his own, using 'his invention' to shake the foundations of the Aristotelian universe.

Pointing the telescope at the Moon, he found it was pockmarked with craters and had mountains and valleys. He also reported that the Sun's face was blemished – prone to disfiguring sunspots!

Turning towards Jupiter he just managed to detect four tiny satellites orbiting it, meaning that it could no longer be said that all the heavenly bodies revolved exclusively, around the Earth. He also observed the phases of Venus, the only straightforward explanation of which was that Venus orbited the Sun and not the Earth.

The Church's response to all this was mixed. On the one hand, the leading Jesuit astronomer of the day, Christopher Clavius, immediately acquired a state-of-the-art telescope and confirmed that Galileo was right about Jupiter's moons and the phases of Venus. The Vatican was not ready, however, to accept all Galileo's conclusions, adopting instead the 'half-way' measure of Tycho Brahe's cosmology. In this system, all the planets except the Earth orbited the Sun!

STELLAR PARALLAX

Galileo certainly knew all about Bruno. But if he was alarmed, he certainly hid it well. Instead, in 1632 along came a new, rather witty book again lampooning Pope Urban. It was this that required Galileo, now an old sick man, to appear a second time before the dreaded Inquisition in Rome.

And this time the verdict was more empathic. Galileo was sentenced to 'abjure' the theory and to keep silent on the subject for the rest of his life, which he was obliged to serve out in… a pleasant country house near Florence.

Galileo's books were put on the index of forbidden reading, where they were to remain for centuries, which seems a ridiculous interference of politics and religion in science.

After all, one respectable argument remaining against putting the Sun at the centre of the universe, which had been discussed by the Ancient Greeks as part of their debate over an Earth-centred universe, was that if the Earth did orbit the Sun, then small changes in the relative position of the stars, known as stellar parallaxes, should have been observable in the sky.

That meant it should surely be possible to measure a shift in the position of a star when observed from the Earth as it orbited the sun, starting at one extreme, and then six months later from the other.

PARALLAX EFFECT

'Parallax effect' is not as complicated as it sounds. It's the effect you get if you look out of a window on one side of a room at say, a tree, noting what the tree is immediately in front of. Then go to the next window along, and see if the tree is still blocking the view of the same thing. Which it won't be. Or you can just hold your hand in front of your eyes and blink each eye alternately.

Looking out when moving between different windows is the equivalent of observing distant stars when the Earth is at opposite ends of its 'hypothetical' orbit around the sun. What's more, the distance between these 'windows', it was recognised, would be vast if Copernicus's theory was correct!

Yet, no matter how hard the astronomers looked, they could not see any change in the relationships of the stars. They looked like they were, indeed, all fixed securely to their crystal sphere. The first time anyone managed to measure any confirming parallax effect wasn't until 300 years later, in 1838.

Appreciation of Parallax went hand in hand with appreciation of perspective, a great Renaissance innovation, revealed in the masterpieces of artists such as Raphael and da Vinci.

Appreciating how the Parallax Effect works requires an understanding of perspective.

VIEWS OF THE MOON

Forget what you may have read about Galileo representing facts and the Church clinging to religious doctrine. In Galileo's day, observational evidence was against him!

That, of course, is only true if you discount the possibility that the stars were much farther away than people then thought.

The scale is, in reality, far outside anything in human experience. Galileo himself hesitated to make such an argument. Equally, many of the features Galileo claimed to have seen on the Moon were belied by the evidence of the naked eye, his observations being 'the result of a fertile brain, rather than a careful eye', as one contemporary astronomer put it. The colourful gas clouds 'revealed' by the telescope were just distorting effects of the lenses.

Another significant, empirical weakness in Copernicus' theory was that it asserted (as did Galileo, even against Kepler's mathematics) that the planets orbit the Sun in perfect circles. The Jesuit astronomers could easily show that this was not in conformity with observations.

But Galileo was not really bothered about the details. What he was proposing through his observations was a fundamental conceptual shift.

No longer was there to be a single reference point – an unambiguous use for words like 'up' and 'down', but from now on he wanted there to be multiple reference 'frames', with familiar terms like being 'at rest' or 'moving' reduced to being only relative terms.

Galileo was, in fact, the first of the Einsteinian relativists. For him, the moon was not floating above the Earth but was held there by a complex web of gravitational forces.

At the time, it might have been easier to take him seriously if he was claiming that the moon really was made of green cheese...

Sir Isaac Newton's theories on gravity were not inspired by an apple falling from a tree.

But not if you were Isaac Newton. It was this esoteric lunar debate that Newton read about as a boy in a book by a young chaplain, John Wilkin, called *The Discovery of a New World* (1638).

It is in this speculation, rather than the supposed experience of seeing an apple fall from a tree, that lies the inspiration of his theory of gravity, as well as the more precise realisation that over a certain distance, the embrace of gravity must become rather less powerful.

Isaac Newton, (1642–1727) was a Christmas Day baby born into a rural family and only his inability to keep track of the cows led to him eventually being allowed to go to Oxford as a kind of assistant scholar to richer students. Once there, he feasted on the knowledge revealed in the libraries, drawing

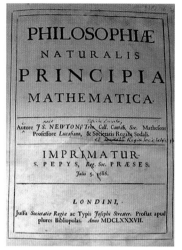

PHILOSOPHIÆ
NATURALIS
PRINCIPIA
MATHEMATICA.

Autore *J S. NEWTON*, *Trin. Coll. Cantab. Soc.* Mathefeos Profeffore Lucafiano, & Societatis Regalis Sodali.

IMPRIMATUR·
S. PEPYS, *Reg. Soc.* PRÆSES.
Julii 5. 1686.

LONDINI,

Juffu *Societatis Regiæ* ac Typis *Jofephi Streater.* Proftat apud plures Bibliopolas. *Anno* MDCLXXXVII.

Newton's own copy of his Principia Mathematica from 1687.

Nonetheless, Newton is sometimes said to have been to science what Euclid was to mathematics. His *Philosophiae Naturalis Principia Mathematica* (1687) systematised the science of mechanics, that is the science of objects and how they move, just as Euclid systematised the study of geometry.

up a list of great questions spanning the whole range of accumulated human knowledge that he intended to investigate.

In the event, he was woefully unsuccessful, scarcely proceeding beyond the first half dozen matters, such as the nature of motion, chemical change, gravity, light – and time.

Despite many secretive years searching for the 'Philosophers Stone' he never managed to come up with that, either.

Both provided the terms and definitions for all who followed.

Newton found it necessary to deal with apparently philosophical issues such as those of the nature of 'space' and of 'true motion' (in particular the views of Descartes) in order to address paradoxes such as the contradictory idea that the Earth could both be 'accelerating' away from the Sun at any moment, and yet also be motionless.

SPIRIT OF THE AGE

If his nostrums of 'Absolute Space' let alone 'Absolute Time' seem to have been collapsed by Relativity theory, Einstein was the first to acknowledge that it was Newton who gave the world the framework for investigations.

Newton and Galileo are such giants of Natural Philosophy that other important figures of the time are easily overlooked. One such is Francis Bacon (1561–1626), another Englishman writing a century or so earlier. However, in many ways, Bacon represents the true spirit of the age better than the secretive and aggressive Newton and the conceited Galileo.

Bacon was a well-connected lawyer, philosopher and politician who (like Machiavelli) produced books of 'advice for rulers', which pleased Queen Elizabeth I well enough for him to be made Lord Chancellor.

Francis Bacon, Viscount St Alban.

MAKING SENSE OF NATURE

Newton's First Law of Motion is Galileo's Principle of Inertia, stating that a body moves in a straight line at uniform velocity unless acted upon.

The principle explains why an object does not fall slightly to the west of the point at which it is dropped, as would appear to be required by the theory that the Earth rotates on its axis. The object retains this rotational motion as it falls.

Newton's two great works are the *Principles of Natural Philosophy* and the *Optics*, the latter also containing ideas concerning subjects as diverse as mechanics, religion and even ethics.

Newton always considered his approach to be empirical, based on observation and measurement, with theory then emerging to explain 'the facts'.

Elements he could not explain, he set aside and noted as such. The force of gravity was one such mystery, yet he explained the mathematical forces produced, and demonstrated how all of nature obeyed these mathematical laws.

He revealed the secrets of the motions of the planets, and the Moon, as well as all the everyday objects around us.

The framework that Newton produced almost single handedly underpins modern physics and shapes the way all of us understand the universe.

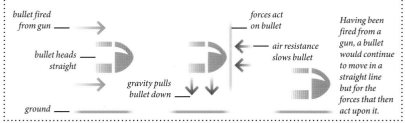

bullet fired from gun

bullet heads straight

gravity pulls bullet down

ground

forces act on bullet

air resistance slows bullet

Having been fired from a gun, a bullet would continue to move in a straight line but for the forces that then act upon it.

Bacon's most important work was in scientific method and how to overcome the so-called problem of induction. This is the scientific habit of drawing general conclusions from limited amounts of data – a practice and form of reasoning that philosophers have long complained is strictly speaking, logically invalid.

It is Bacon who really represents the spirit of the New Age, so let's start with a closer look at this under-rated thinker. Francis Bacon is conventionally counted as the first of the British 'empiricists'.

Francis Bacon considered scientific questions such as the way the Sun provides heat and light.

He epitomises the new ideas of scientific method, and devoted himself to developing a system combining data drawn from experience with a form of negative reasoning sometimes referred to as 'eliminative induction'.

This was supposed to provide a solid base for certain knowledge, while allowing the widest possible range to ideas and research.

For example, scientists looking into the relationship between heat and luminosity, he suggested, should consider cases where heat is present, such as in the Sun's rays, and where it is absent, such as in phosphorescence. They can then try to develop an hypothesis to make sense of the evidence.

The approach may reflect Bacon's legal interests, in that English Common Law develops 'inductively', as it were, from the accumulation of past case law, before being applied as established doctrine to new cases.

Bacon dismissed the long-held philosophical assumption (epitomised by Plato) that it is thorough careful

Bacon suggested that scientists should study luminosity in the absence of heat, as demonstrated by this Blue Jellyfish.

examination of the meaning of words that real knowledge can be obtained, pointing out that this was like spinning a web inside your own head.

Nor did he think much of Aristotle's method of hoovering up empirical data and then expecting the truth to emerge almost mechanically.

Instead, Bacon stressed the need for a theoretical insight that will make sense of the mass (indeed, 'mess', too) of data.

NATURAL IDOLS

In his book, the Novum Organum *(1620, usually translated as the* New Organon, *an Organon being merely a collection of philosophical writings), which is his most important book, despite being one he would never finish, Bacon offers four 'idols' to guide philosophical investigations of the natural world.*

THE FOUR IDOLS

▪ The idols of the tribe. These are innate tendencies to which we all fall prey, such as the tendency to see order and patterns in things where order and patterns do not exist, or simply to be misled by our senses. For example, hands that are cold from ice or snow, will perceive the temperature of water to be higher than it really is.

The idols of the cave focussed on preconceptions.

Ice and snow affect the perception of heat.

▪ The idols of the cave. These are errors particular to individuals (rather than collectively held) and depend on each person's own experiences and cultural bound. It is the tendency to judge new experiences in the light of past experiences, and to view everything through a filter of preconceptions.

Words and language were at the heart of the idols of the marketplace.

■ The idols of the market place. These are the errors that arise through social interaction, quintessentially through the use and abuse of words and language. Bacon particularly warns against the use of jargon, and decries the habit of

Elaborate stories were behind the idols of the theatre.

experts of all kinds creating new names and conjuring up new entities.

■ The idols of the theatre. This is the human tendency to enjoy a grand story, and thus to explain many events by reference to one or two instances that seem to us to offer an aesthetically pleasing explanation. Social science offers many such explanations. We might like to think that being poor and not having access to education 'explained' why little Johnny became a bank robber, but in actual fact, there are any number of equally poor and uneducated children who took different decisions and paths.

Bacon tells us that: 'Those who have handled sciences have been either men of experiment or men of dogmas.

'The men of experiment are like the ant, they only collect and use; the reasoners resemble spiders, who make cobwebs out of their own substance.

'But the bee takes a middle course: it gathers its material from the flowers of the garden and of the field, but transforms and digests it by a power of its own. Not unlike this is the true business of philosophy; for it neither relies solely or chiefly on the powers of the mind, nor does it take the matter which it gathers from natural history and mechanical experiments and lay it up in the memory whole, as it finds it, but lays it up in the understanding altered and digested.

'Therefore from a closer and purer league between these two faculties, the experimental and the rational (such as has never yet been made), much may be hoped.'

Bacon described dogmatic thinkers as being like spiders.

Bacon believed that true philosophers were like honey bees.

ANT AND BEE

Bacon also offers several analogies of his own to demonstrate how he thinks human knowledge should advance. Philosophers, like Plato. who looked inwards for knowledge, he says are like spiders who spin elaborate webs out of material all of which necessarily comes only from within their own minds.

On the other hand, those who look at the evidence, as to some extent Aristotle did, he says are like ants forever collecting tiny fragments and sticking them together into a great heap of information.

The true philosopher, says Bacon, is like a honey bee. Bees gather the ingredients they need from the natural word, but then transform it into the mathematically perfect honeycombs and yummy honey itself.

THE NEW ORGANON, 1620

Francis Bacon, as mentioned previously, was very active politically, as were all of the great thinkers at this time. During the Renaissance period in Europe, in parallel with the rise of science, came a shift away from the study of God towards the study of humanity.

There was interest in the relationship of humans to nature, a confidence in the judgements and the abilities of the human mind, and a conviction that it was better to consider ethical issues from the point of view of human interests than from that of some supposed divinity. Petrach (born 1304) is generally considered the first humanist, while Erasmus (born 1466) is counted as its greatest exponent.

But it is Machiavelli who is certainly the most famous political philosopher of this time.

Machiavelli's method is rather like Francis Bacon's – but applied to society. He looks through history for examples of certain incidents, and notes the consequences, good or bad, for the ruler involved.

He then forms a hypothesis, which is tested and either confirmed or disproved. It is in this sense that Machiavelli then sets out the means to achieve certain ends,

Statue of Niccolo Machiavelli at the Uffizi Gallery in Florence, Italy.

A 1646 edition of The Prince *by Niccolo Machiavelli.*

irrespective of any virtue or merit in those ambitions.

Machiavelli's focus is on how to secure political success. It's scarcely surprising that ambitious politicians, including the likes of the President of the United States, Barack Obama, still read his works.

You might think that the first question to ask is 'how?', but really the fist thing to decide is 'what?'. What counts as success? Machiavelli offers three possible domains: national security, national independence and a strong constitution. And to achieve these, the end, famously, always justifies the means.

As many politicians erroneously reason, if the end is good, then the means used to achieve it scarcely matter. Machiavelli wrote two classic texts: *The Prince* and *The Discourses*, a longer, less well-known work that offers a more nuanced view.

In this work, the emphasis is placed on the division of powers and protecting and upholding the constitution.

SOCIAL IDEALS

Sixteenth-century Italy benefited from several specific features that made it, like Greece centuries before, fertile ground for the arts, for philosophy and for political thinking.

It was wealthy and politically diverse with a sophisticated, secular culture. City states or 'communes' presided over by their own 'princes' created a patchwork of political parties, such as the oligarchy in Venice and the tyranny in Milan and the democracy in Florence.

Machiavelli was arrested and tortured during upheavals in Florence.

Florence is the magnificent Italian city where Dante wrote not only of his vision of hell, the *Inferno*, but also about the politics of human society.

Considering the question, 'Why should people want to live peacefully and collectively together, when they could often gain more by striking out alone, or by competing against one another?' Dante supposes that social life is the best way for people to develop their potential in general and their rational nature in particular.

Niccolò Machiavelli, a middle-ranking civil servant who had worked for the new Florentine democracy, took a different approach.

Machiavelli is not idealistic, rather he considers himself focussed entirely on practical politics, and in his books makes frequent reference to being involved with the 'real issues' in government.

In his case, this included being arrested and tortured during the purge following the collapse of the Florentine democracy and the Medicis' attempt to return, the Medicis being the ruling family in Florence, their name a byword for over-indulgence and corruption.

The punishment
of flatterers, a
scene from Dante's
Inferno.

Only when finally acquitted was he able to retire from the administration and concentrate on writing up his political ideas. This then is the backdrop to two of the most influential – and controversial – political works ever written, *Il principo (The Prince)* and *Discorsi sopra la prima deca di Tito Livio (Discourses on the first Ten Books of Titus Livy,* usually known as *The Discourses).*

If everyday life in Machiavelli's Italy was very different from that in today's industrial, high-tech world, his ideas are still, sometimes strikingly, relevant. In 16th-century Italy, society and power were split between three groups: the land and peasantry, industry (such as it was), and the bureaucracy, of which Machiavelli had been a member.

This is a surprisingly timeless arrangement. Even Machiavelli's discussion of military adventures can be taken as a metaphor for the strategies and effects of economic competition today, in the manner of *The Art of War,* an ancient Chinese text attributed to Sun Tzu, a high-ranking military general, strategist and tactician.

Perhaps Machiavelli's most controversial and unscrupulous claim is that if a prince must choose to be either feared or loved, it is better that he be feared, for 'love is held by a chain

Florence in Tuscany, Italy, where Dante and Machiavelli wrote their seminal works.

of obligation which [for] men, being selfish, is broken whenever it serves their purpose; but fear is maintained by a dread of punishment which never fails'. In this sense, he is Thomas Hobbes a century later, who sees fear as essential to social order, or even Mao Zedong in the 20th century, who writes in the *Red Book* that power comes out of the barrel of a gun. Nonetheless, Machiavelli's advice for princes includes the guidance that when:

Mao Zedong believed that power came from the barrel of a gun.

'... a Prince is obliged to take the life of anyone, let him do so when there is a proper justification and manifest reason for it; but above all he must abstain from taking the property of others, for men forget more easily the death of their father than the loss of their patrimony.'

Of course, as Machiavelli notes: 'the pretexts for seizing property are never wanting, and one who begins to live by rapine will always find some reason for taking the goods of others, whereas causes for taking life are more fleeting.'

PERILS OF INJUSTICE

Actually, much of Machiavelli's notoriety probably relates to his attacks on the Church. He blames the Bishop of Rome (the pope) for the political ruin of Italy, even though, on his deathbed, he asked for – and received – absolution.

This slightly hypocritical tactic is, of course, very much in keeping with Machiavelli's political philosophy. Machiavelli's real attitude to Christianity can be seen when he writes: 'Our religion has glorified humble and contemplative men, rather than men of action. It has assigned as man's highest good humility, abnegation, and contempt for mundane things... '

Instead, the advice Machiavelli offers to would-be rulers in Renaissance Europe is to transcend conventional values, especially the Christian ones, and follow a separate, privileged ethic of rulers.

Naturally, this is not just a Machiavellian notion – even Plato allowed it in his 'noble lie', which he used to explain the different upbringing and roles of the citizens.

Corruption in elections, and the use of violence and deceit to manipulate opinion is something of a political constant, and was particularly obvious in the affairs of the papacy. Machiavelli is simply presenting plainly a policy that most governments follow but prefer to keep veiled and ambiguous.

Many people misunderstand Machiavelli. He is not saying 'might is right', far less 'anything goes' in government. Instead, one of his most consistent themes is the perils of ignoring injustice.

He urges princes to 'consider how important it is for every republic and every prince to take account of such offences, not only when an injury is done to a whole people but also when it affects an individual.'

The cathedral complex in Florence at sunset.

Illustrative of this is his retelling of the story of the Greek noble, Pausanias, who was brutally raped by one of the king's other favourites. When the attacker was later promoted, the victim vented his anger against the king by killing him, even though this involved 'all manner of dangers' and inevitably ensured Pausanias' own downfall.

Machiavelli tells the story to demonstrate that it is not in the prince's interests to allow the injustice. We might say that oppressing a minority is not in the interests of the state, as such groups may eventually turn to violence – even if they cannot win through such means.

What of that other great political philosopher, Thomas Hobbes? Hobbes' views are set out in the *Leviathan*, published in 1651 and written during the English Civil War. The full title is *Leviathan or The Matter, Forme and Power of a Common Wealth Ecclesiasticall and Civil*.

Thomas Hobbes's Leviathan *was written during great turmoil in England when Oliver Cromwell forcefully disbanded Parliament.*

Non est potestas Super Terram quæ Comparetur ei Iob. 41 24

The frontispiece of the book Leviathan by Thomas Hobbes.

A leviathan is a kind of sea monster, an odd title and metaphor for Hobbes to use. But then, his books are a strange mixture of law, religious enthusiasm and political iconoclasm.

There is a psychological undertone of guilt reminiscent of St Augustine a thousand years before, who devoted thousands of pages to alternately apologising and blaming himself for the wickedness that led him to steal pears and, even worse, to enjoy them!

Psychology, then, is at the heart of Thomas Hobbes' theorising, but it is Hobbes' political theory, the first significant one since Machiavelli's, that is the most interesting and, historically, the most important.

This is presented, in the manner of geometry, by outlining some baseline assumptions, almost axioms. One is that people are just machines, driven to actions by what he terms 'appetites' and 'aversions'.

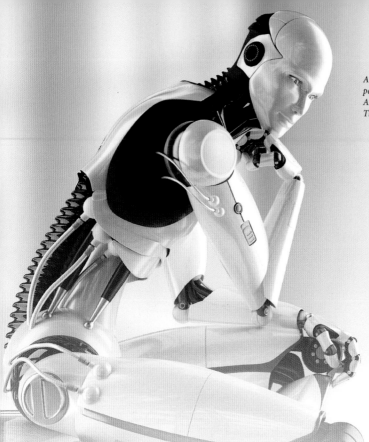

A modern automaton poses in the manner of Auguste Rodin's 'The Thinker' statue.

'These small beginnings of Motion within the body of Man, before they appear in walking, speaking, striking, and other visible actions are commonly called ENDEAVOUR. This Endeavour, when it is toward something, is called APPETITE or DESIRE; the latter, being the general name, and the other often times restrained to signify the Desire of Food, namely Hunger and Thirst. And when the Endeavour is fromward something, it is generally called AVERSION,' is how Hobbes sums it up.

These days, we often wonder if

computers are really alive, but in Hobbes' time, people wondered whether automata, the clockwork mechanisms that were such a great feature of the period, appearing like outrageous children's toys on the church steeples of the richest towns, were artificially alive.

Hobbes says that the motions of automata are no more mindless than the motions of the animal or human beings, and the human being is no more free to direct its impulses than the machine is.

Some, but not many, of these 'motions' are innate, the rest are the result of experience. Everyone seeks to fulfil these appetites, varying only in degree and particular taste.

Hobbes says the 'human machine' is programmed to direct its energies selfishly. He doubts if it is ever possible for human beings to act altruistically, and even apparently benevolent action is actually self-serving, perhaps an attempt to make those who act in this way feel good about themselves. Instead, for human beings, 'in the first place, I put for a general inclination of all mankind, a perpetual and restless desire after Power, that ceaseth only in Death.'

This psychological theory of human motivation is often associated with the writings of Nietzsche, sometimes with Hegel, but it is Hobbes who puts it so much more convincingly and elegantly 200 years earlier.

This early 17th-century novelty automaton trundled forward and the goddess Diana could even fire arrows.

CHAPTER 5

ENLIGHTENMENT, PHILOSOPHY AND THE RISE OF SCIENCE

'... *A man may imagine things that are false, but he can only understand things that are true, for if the things be false, the apprehension of them is not understanding.*'

Isaac Newton

Sir Isaac Newton using a prism to study the constituent colours of sunlight.

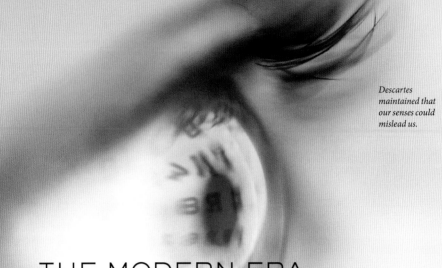

Descartes maintained that our senses could mislead us.

THE MODERN ERA

'Modern philosophy', a term by which the academic philosophers mean 'real philosophy', rather than anything particularly modern, is conventionally taken to start in the 17th century with the French polymath, René Descartes.

Descartes' stated aim (by no means original) was to bring to philosophy the rigour and certainty of mathematics. His famous dictum 'I think therefore I am' (in Latin, *cogito ergo sum*) has acted as a motto for philosophers ever since.

It is probably the most famous argument of them all. Descartes claims that from it, from just this one golden nugget of logical certainty, he can dispel all the demons of doubt that otherwise plague philosophical reasoning.

For rationalists', such as Descartes, the essential starting point is that human perception is always potentially misleading.

'The senses deceive from time to time, and it is prudent never to trust wholly those who have deceived us even once.'

René Descartes

THE *COGITO*

The *Cogito* is a very short argument.
It has several forms but the best known is:

I think
Therefore
I am

In Latin it runs: *cogito, ergo, sum*. The Latin
version, however, is not the original one at
all. For such a short argument, it is actually
very unclear. The way that Descartes was
using it is actually more like this than the
'short version' implies.

I am aware of thoughts
Only something that exists can think
Therefore: Every time I am aware
of my thoughts, I know that I exist.

*Sculptor Auguste
Rodin's 'The
Thinker' statue.*

Instead, rationalism is about
appealing to intellectual and deductive
reason as the source of knowledge
or justification, as opposed to sense
experience. The approach is associated
with the introduction of mathematical
methods into philosophy and contrasts
with empiricism, the view that the
source of all knowledge is sense
experience and sensory perception.

Gottfried Leibniz, German philosopher and mathematician.

The school of rationalism is sometimes called Continental Rationalism because its key figures – Descartes, Leibniz and Spinoza – were continental Europeans. Yet the great British thinker, Isaac Newton, active in the same period, is also very much a rationalist, and far from being a 'British Empiricist', so these geographical distinctions should not be taken too far.

A point not often noted about these three giants of Continental Rationalism, is that all of them died rather ignominiously. Descartes caught pneumonia and died far from home in Sweden, for him an unloved land of snow and ice. Spinoza died

GOTTFRIED WILHELM LEIBNIZ.

aged just 44, with his books on the Church's banned lists, and Leibniz's last days were filled by controversies about whether or not he had stolen other people's ideas. Only Leibniz's secretary attended his funeral and his grave was left unmarked for the next 50 years. All three thinkers were suspected of being involved in black magic – and maybe politics, too!

Rationalism, it might seem, does not pay, but then rationalism is all about ideas, and ideas are something that these philosophers certainly had in spades.

THE CONTINENTAL RATIONALISTS

- 1596 Rene Descartes is born in La Haye, France.
- 1632 Baruch Spinoza is born in Amsterdam, Holland.
- 1646 Gottfried Leibniz is born in Leipzig, Germany.
- 1637 Descartes publishes his *Discourse on Method*, an unusual work notable for its engaging first-person style. This novelty, however, had less to do with Descartes' modernity than with the *Discourses* being basically the foreword for a much longer, conventional book, which never appeared.

Baruch de Spinoza, Dutch philosopher.

- 1670 Spinoza's *Tractatus* appears. Seven years later, his *Ethics* is published posthumously.
- 1685 Leibniz wrote mostly short essays and letters, and only one book-length work, the *Theodicy*, was published in his lifetime. His *Discourse on Metaphysics* came out in 1685, followed in 1710 by the *Theodicy* and in 1714 by the *Monadology*.

MIND AND MATTER

Descartes' new geometry of knowledge is based on identifying a very few basic certainties, labelling them as clear truths and then enlarging and expanding on them.

For example, having discovered it to be 'impossible' to doubt the existence of his thoughts but entirely possible to imagine the non-existence of his body, Descartes concludes that the world consists of two different kinds of entity: mind and matter. Mind – the 'thing that thinks' – is a separate substance, entirely independent of the body.

Descartes' famous speculation is that it is quite possible to dream you are sitting by a nice warm fire in a medieval stove room, without actually being there – you might just be tucked up in bed. Since we can be wrong about everything, he says, only one thing is

Wherever you may be, Descartes says your awareness of your thoughts is certain.

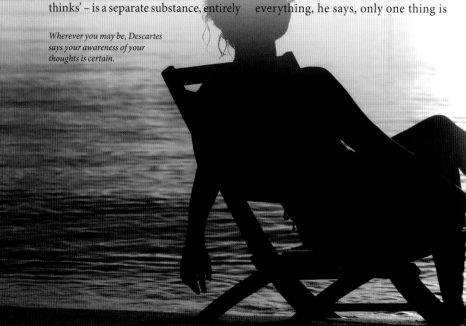

left that we can't be mistaken about, and that is that if you think you are in a nice warm oven room, you are indeed thinking that, irrespective of whether you are there, or you are tucked up in bed, or you are dozing on a beach. Your awareness of your thoughts is direct and certain.

This idea was by no means new. In fact, Descartes was rather literally restating an old Catholic view, put by Saint Augustine, who in turn was repeating views to be found in Aristotle.

Augustine had taught that: 'He who is not can certainly not be deceived; therefore, if I am deceived, I am.'

As befits one educated under stern and orthodox Jesuit masters, Descartes obediently repeats many of Saint Augustine's credos in his philosophy. How 'modern' is that? Not very, and nor is there really an effort to test the old Church teachings. The 'method of doubt', crucially, does not include doubting those opinions that appear particularly plausible.

*Was the fate of
the world really
in God's hands?*

DIVINE REVELATION

*For Saint Augustine, it seemed reasonable to regularly bridge gaps in arguments
by announcing the assistance of 'divine revelation' and Descartes follows suit,
putting limits on scepticism by saying that God would not allow certain things.*

More importantly, he argues that all that appears obvious to us – 'everything perceived clearly and distinctly' – must be true.

In many ways, it makes sense to say that if things appear very obviously to be the case, there is no need to 'probe them'. Euclid, remember, started off his geometry with certain axioms, and had he not done so, he could not have produced any of his interesting and powerful theorems.

On the other hand, the method of relying on common sense or, to use Descartes phrase, 'our natural light', leaves open the possibility for others to see by the natural light truths that we ourselves might be inclined to doubt. Who is to judge what is obvious?

Consciousness, thoughts, minds – none of these terms are very well defined or understood even today. Clearly, Descartes has in mind something very close to the traditional Christian notion of eternal souls.

Indeed, Descartes (who loved to investigate the workings of animal and human bodies and conducted many cruel experiments on animals) claimed to have discovered a small gland, the pineal gland, in the human body, that was, he said, where the soul lived. From here the gland directed the operations of the rest of the body, although not by biochemical or physical means.

As mentioned, one problem is that it seems the thinking things and the material bodies can never interact. Descartes toyed with the idea that a strange influence of the soul on particles passing through the gland could yet have a guiding effect. And then there was the 'synchronized clocks' possibility: that a divine providence should have arranged the universe so that when, for example, you (meaning your mind) wants to eat, your body also wants to eat. In effect, yes, God to the rescue.

Descartes claimed to have found the part of the brain where the soul lived.

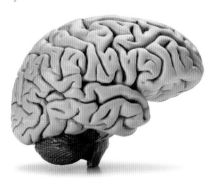

Alas, there is no space in Descartes' system for animals to have souls or indeed feelings. He insists that animals are but unconscious brutes, mere machines. Descartes would cut up dogs and monkeys and ignore their cries as simply the whirring of wheels in an intricate piece of machinery.

Descartes explains also that philosophy is 'like a tree' with metaphysics being the roots, physics (what we would call science) being the main trunk, and all the other human studies being the branches. This broad spread of inquiry, he adds, has just three main sources: medicine, mechanics and morals. Medicine, mechanics and morals? Morals as a branch of physics? Here, the Cartesian philosopher seems to be, just as his accusers regularly said, intent on reducing the world to a machine.

There is a peculiar story told about Descartes, one of several urban myths,

Descartes compared philosophy to the parts of a great tree.

that appears to have circulated soon after his death in 1650. The story concerns his daughter Francine. Now Descartes never married, but he did have an affair with Helena, a woman who worked in a bookshop that he lodged over in Amsterdam – and Francine was the result.

Philosophers are not particularly successful in terms of conventional family relationships. Spinoza, Leibniz and Descartes were all bachelors. If Socrates seems to have got on passably well with his wife, Xanthippe (40 years his junior, mind you…), Aristotle's influential view that women are a kind of domestic cattle that live in the house reveals a rather nasty assumption of superiority

Descartes' house in Amsterdam, Netherlands.

amongst the male philosophers.

The fact is that Descartes had a daughter with a young woman who worked in the bookshop. Actually, and perhaps surprisingly in view of his other attitudes, he seems to have been very fond of both of them and to have planned to look after both his lover and their child in a quiet corner of Holland.

Descartes' plan was that they would use the 'cover story' that Helena was Descartes' servant and Francine was his niece. You can often read that Descartes had 'an illegitimate child' with a servant, which is quite misleading.

Alas, the young child died of scarlet fever and four years later the records show Helena married a local innkeeper.

Queen Christina of Sweden brought Descartes to Stockholm to teach philosophy.

Descartes comes across as a braggart and even an egomaniac in some respects, yet history also records that he provided the 1000-guilder dowry for Helena's wedding and stayed in the area for a number of years pursuing his researches, including his life-long passion for automata. Until, that is, being summoned by the Queen of Sweden to teach philosophy.

DESCARTES' LIVING STATUES

Descartes, it is known, was fascinated by automata. But here's a story which I stress, may or may not be true. But then how much in philosophy is? It seems that Descartes told the crew of the boat that was to take him to Sweden that he would be travelling with his young daughter (despite this being some years after her death) and that he did not wish to be disturbed under any circumstances.

During the voyage, across the North Sea, the boat was caught in a particularly dreadful storm and the crew decided that, despite Descartes instruction not to enter his quarters, they had to warn him about preparing for a possible emergency evacuation of the ship.

However, when they burst through Descartes' door they found no sign of him, far less his daughter, but they did find a large, sinister-looking black trunk. It seems that the sailors, already consumed by curiosity, could not restrain themselves now from forcing this open and taking a look inside.

On opening the case they were astonished to find an incredibly lifelike, full-sized doll of a lovely young girl... Francine. Touching it, their astonishment turned to terror when the doll sat upright and turned its eyes to look at them! It was an magnificently fine, beautifully constructed automaton.

They showed what they had discovered to the captain and he, having never seen anything like it before, suspected it might be a work of black magic and ordered it to thrown overboard into the waters of the North Sea. It was never seen again.

A 'writing' automaton doll.

METHOD OF DOUBT

*Descartes is generally considered a much greater philosopher by
the English and the Americans than he is by his fellow countrymen.
The French seem to know him better, recognising that, in many ways,
Descartes' philosophy rests on borrowed ideas extended ineffectually.*

*Castle 'Tre Kronor' in Stockholm
as it appeared in 1661.*

He is praised for his 'Method of Doubt' – but this is an old story in philosophy. The Ancient Sceptics doubted far more vigorously and seriously than Descartes.

By creating a rigid divide between mind and matter in his philosophy, Descartes was really only restating one of the principles of the Catholic philosophers. Although he claimed through his philosophy finally to demonstrate logically the existence of God, in practice he really ushered in a period of rampant materialism.

On the other hand, Descartes did leave a very real body of ideas and insights in other less obviously philosophical areas, not least his work in mathematics. Had it not been for the demands of the Queen of Sweden for philosophy lessons, he might have achieved much more, too.

Descartes died only a few years after publication of the *Meditations,* in that 'land of bears between rocks and ice' as he describes it unfondly. He was intent on his writings to the last but these

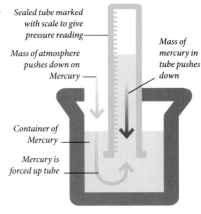

Sealed tube marked with scale to give pressure reading

Mass of atmosphere pushes down on Mercury

Mass of mercury in tube pushes down

Container of Mercury

Mercury is forced up tube

In Stockholm, Descartes conducted experiments with a Torricelian barometer, as in the above diagram, to try to establish whether air pressure could be used to forecast weather patterns.

were not, as might be assumed by those reared on the Cartesian legend, great philosophical treatises. What he was actually finishing was a comedy and a ballet for the Swedish Queen and her Courtiers' amusement.

Fortunately, most philosophers are usually remembered for their ideas rather than their acts. This historical courtesy has served the second great rationalist thinker, Baruch Spinoza, particularly well.

Spinoza's work turned him into something of an outcast.

THE ONE THING

What is the true story of Spinoza? The Dutch philosopher, Jewish by origin although unceremoniously ejected from his sect presumably for his disgraceful philosophical theories, shared something of Descartes' and Leibniz's style and ambition.

The difference was that Spinoza focused on the idea that the universe consists of just one thing, proposing in his writing that: 'There is only one substance, and that substance we can conceive of as either Nature or God.' In this sense, Spinoza unifies the very different approaches of his contemporaries. The split Descartes created between mind and matter, Spinoza hopes is thus healed.

Spinoza only published two books in his lifetime. The first was *The Principles of Descartes' Philosophy,* with a foreword briskly stepping though Descartes' core ideas and rejecting each one in turn. Spinoza does not think that there are two distinct entities, mind and matter, nor that human beings have 'free will', nor will he have it that there is anything beyond human understanding.

This book is not much read anyway, Spinoza's reputation resting more on his *Tractatus Theologico-Politicius* ('A Theologico-Political Treatise'). From the vantage point of today it looks like a devotional work, but he was sufficiently concerned about being accused of heresy to falsify the book details in a bid to remain anonymous.

Amongst other innovations, the *Tractatus* treats the Bible as a human-made text like any other, open to doubt and requiring deconstruction. Indeed, the Tractatus was immediately controversial and when Spinoza was 'unmasked' as the author, he became much reviled.

Even after Spinoza's death, when his friends planned to publish some of his

other writings, they thought it wise to conceal his authorship by crediting the books, to 'BDS' . Thus one of the foundation 'modern' texts of Western philosophy, Spinoza's 'masterpiece', *Ethics, Demonstrated in Geometrical Order* (usually just the *Ethics*), had to be published, in effect, anonymously.

The 17th-century New Church in the Hague, Netherlands – Spinoza is buried in the garden.

Spinoza's views on God and heaven were highly controversial during his lifetime.

The *Ethics*, like Descartes' *Meditations*, is fundamentally concerned to provide a logical basis for believing in God, a strategy that you might think religious authorities would be favourable towards, but on the contrary, they hated it.

Spinoza's God is stripped of so many attributes (such as having wishes, ideas or preferences) that for many, at the time, it was considered to be atheism by another name, and to substantiate the worst things that his countrymen had said about him.

Quite what these bad things were, no one seems to know, but Spinoza was excommunicated from his Jewish synagogue at the age of 24.

The official decree, or '*cherem*', throwing

Spinoza was excommunicated from his synagogue.

him out speaks of 'evil opinions and acts', 'abominable heresies' and 'monstrous deeds'. No specific deeds are actually recorded and philosophers have speculated ever since about what occasioned such hostility.

One theory is that he offended the Jewish community in Amsterdam by reviving the vexed debate over what happened to the soul after death, an issue that the locals had only finally been able to lay to rest after asking the Jewish community in Venice for a ruling.

For Christians, it is individual humans who survive, taking their virtues and vices to the pearly gates for Saint Peter to evaluate.

The Great Flood is as much a concern as what's for supper.

WORRY ABOUT EVERYTHING EQUALLY

One of Spinoza's impeccably logical arguments is that it is irrational to worry less about past misfortunes (say, the Great Flood), than about future problems (say, not having any food for supper).

How can this approach make sense? The reason is, at least for Spinoza, that everything is already determined.

You imagine that you can still act to save yourself from being hungry this evening, but in fact, if you are fated to have no supper, then that is what will happen. Similarly, the fact that you can't do a thing about the Great Flood is splendidly irrelevant to whether you judge it to have been very bad news for the people of the time.

THE THIRD MAN

Philosophy has long recognised that the Christians' idea of very literal human survival seems impossible, and philosophers developed a more subtle view on the matter.

The notion, sometimes attributed to Maimonides, is that the only thing that survives the death of the body is 'knowledge', or more precisely knowledge of God. Spinoza's views seem to have been similar.

'I like mathematics because it is not human and has nothing particular to do with this planet or with the whole accidental universe – because, like Spinoza's God, it won't love us in return.'

Bertrand Russell

Entrance to the Heilige Geesthofje in The Hague, Netherlands, where Spinoza died.

Silk cocoons with silk worm on mulberry leaves.

Our third great rationalist, Leibniz, visited Spinoza in The Hague in 1676. The two men discussed philosophy together over several days.

'Although there is no written record of their conversation, it seems likely that these discussions were among the most rewarding in the whole history of philosophy,' writes one typical contemporary account of the meeting.

Alas, the reality is as ever rather different. Spinoza becoming unfashionable, Leibniz swiftly distanced himself from him and even minimised Spinoza's conversation as consisting mainly of 'political anecdotes'!

This sneaky behaviour is all too typical of Gottfried Leibniz. The man was clearly very brilliant – another polymath – and interested not only in what we would today call philosophy but more or less all natural phenomena and questions. But he was also deeply flawed.

For example, inspired by the ancient Chinese interest in duality, exemplified by the hexagrams of the I Ching, he tried, despite the absence of modern technologies, to construct a binary computer; he actually constructed a steam powered carriage that he claimed went considerable distances at high speeds, and he established a reasonably successful business producing – with silk worms – silk in Europe.

Philosophically, his project to make the universe rational by representing knowledge as simple statements ('atomic facts') veered into mysticism with his incomprehensible account of what he called 'monads'.

These are perhaps the most mysterious objects ever created in philosophy – they have no parts, hence 'atomic', are windowless and colourless (light neither enters nor leaves), and are living centres of energy. His writings offer clues rather than explanations:

'I maintain also that substances, whether material or immaterial, cannot be conceived in their bare essence without any activity, activity being of the essence of substance in general.'

And also:

'The ultimate reason of things must lie in a necessary substance, in which the differentiation of the changes only exists eminently as in their source; and this is what we call God.'

The bottom line with the monads, he explains, is that they can never be seen, and can only be approached through pure logic.

Leibniz is that rare thing, a philosopher whose parents were philosophers – his

father was a lecturer of moral philosophy. Partly because of his parents' academic background, Leibniz had mastered Latin when he was eight and started learning Greek at age 12. Naturally, logic followed soon after.

Leibniz turned down a university job in law, preferring to work for the nobility of Hanover, just as Spinoza, for all the reports of how this great thinker was forced to grind spectacle lenses, turned down an academic job at Heidelberg, one of Europe's best universities at the time.

In sum, Leibniz was one of the period's most inventive minds, but there is still some doubt about the extent to which his discoveries were genuine, as opposed to being borrowed and hyped. Among the triumphs he claimed was a calculating machine that was designed to perform the operations of multiplication, addition and subtraction, division and root extraction.

Leibniz studied law at the University of Altdorf in Nürnberg but declined an offer to take up a post there.

Leibniz's machine was displayed at the Academy of Paris and to the Royal Society of London. With this achievement, he was elected at the latter society as a fellow in April in 1673. Leibniz's achievement is important, but his machine was closely based on Pascal's calculator.

Leibniz also thought that it was possible and desirable to construct an artificial language to better exhibit the logical form of arguments. Like many other philosophers before and since, he sought to make the world more rational, by rearranging the universe into fundamental and eternal 'simple facts', logical atoms as Bertrand Russell similarly describes them.

These are the ultimate building blocks of reality, the 'monads' as Leibniz calls them. Knowledge is essentially a matter of analyzing these 'building blocks' of reality in order to explain reality and understand the meaningfulness of language.

Leibniz summed up this view when he wrote that:

'Languages are the best mirror of the human mind, and that a precise analysis of the significations of words would tell us more than anything else about the operations of the understanding.'

Leibniz's Staffelwalze, ('Stepped Reckoner') could perform all four arithmetic operations; addition, subtraction, multiplication and division.

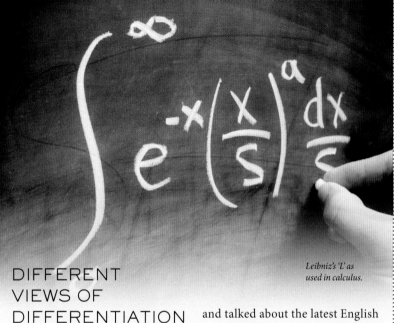

$$\int_{0}^{\infty} e^{-x} \left(\frac{x}{s}\right)^{a} \frac{dx}{s}$$

Leibniz's 'L' as used in calculus.

DIFFERENT VIEWS OF DIFFERENTIATION

The controversy over who invented the calculator was as nought compared to whether it was Leibniz or Newton who invented calculus.

The facts are unclear, although Leibniz went on a short trip to London before his arrival in Hanover in 1676. During this trip, Leibniz met grandees of the Royal Society and talked about the latest English thinking on the matter. Newton always accused Leibniz of stealing his unpublished work on calculus, but then Newton accused everyone of trying to steal his ideas.

The one thing Leibniz can claim is the right to the elongated 'L' of the integral in calculus. In typical style this was intended to compliment him, but it also has a simple elegance.

LEIBNIZ'S PRINCIPLES

In long essays such as the Discourse on Metaphysics, *(1666) and the* General Inquiries
(1681) as well as the Monadology *(1714), Leibniz explores his theory and describes
possible complex arrangements of his monads.*

His conclusion from all this was that the world was in fact perfect, the 'best of all possible worlds' as Voltaire sarcastically put it, and needed no supervision from God or anyone else.

Leibniz's mind threw out ideas all the time, from practical inventions like a steam powered coach (which some accounts say was actually made and achieved great speeds) to his investigations of binary numbers – investigations often generously counted as foreshadowing the inventions of the digital computer.

But within philosophy, he offers several apparently self-evident principles. There is the principle of sufficient reason.

The law of non-contradiction says that water cannot flow both downhill and uphill.

This states that, in the case of any positive truth, there is some reason for it, i.e. there is some sort of explanation, known or unknown, for everything. The world does not seem to contain within itself the reason for its own existence. Therefore, God exists.

Then there is the law of non-contradiction. This says that there are an infinite number of infinitely complex and complete concepts, all considered as possibly existent substances, with none having any particular 'right' to exist over another. There is one limit: each substance must not just be possible in isolation but must be possible together, the universe as a whole forming a vast, consistent, non-contradictory system. For example, God could not create a universe in which water flows both downhill and uphill.

And then there is the principle of the identity of indiscernibles. This states that no two distinct things can exactly resemble each other. It is often referred to as 'Leibniz's Law' and is typically understood to mean that no two objects have exactly the same properties.

In the *Monadology*, Leibniz offers a view inspired by the new microworlds revealed by the microscope:

'*Thus each organized body of all living beings is a kind of divine machine or natural automaton, which infinitely surpasses all artificial automata.*

'*For a machine constructed by man's art is not a machine in each of its parts. For example, the tooth of a brass wheel has parts or fragments which, for us, are no longer artificial things, and no longer have any marks to indicate the machine for whose use the wheel was intended. But natural machines, that is, living bodies, are still machines in their least parts, to infinity. This is the difference between nature and art, that is, between divine art and our art.*'

Microscopic scientific study began to align science and philosophy.

Ultimately, Leibniz's universe consists only of God and the indivisible, immaterial, soul-like entities called 'monads'. Space, time, cause-and-effect, material objects, and so on, are all illusions. Yet these illusions in some sense reflect the true nature of the universe at a more fundamental level.

Descartes, Spinoza and Leibniz are the great names of rationalist philosophy – but the great rationalist, in truth, is the thinker whose success was so great that he removed himself 'outside' the realms of philosophy and became instead the founding figure of a new kind of science, called Physics.

This thinker was the son of an English farmer called Isaac Newton. Both the son and the father shared the same name, but it would never cause any confusion because Isaac senior died just before Isaac junior was born.

An 18th-century engraving
of Sir Isaac Newton.

The important point, though, is that the future mathematics genius could hardly have had a background more different to the other rationalist philosophers of the age. Yet he was very much concerned in the same logical-mathematical enterprise as the three continentals.

THE FIRST SCIENTIST

To Newton we owe the foundations of science and he counts as the first true scientist – all before were philosophers of nature. Newton painstakingly unlocked the secrets of the universe, genuinely taking nothing for granted, nothing as certain that he had not seen probed.

His book, *Philosophiæ Naturalis Principia Mathematica,* systematised the science of mechanics, that is of objects and how they move, just as Euclid's 'Elements' had systematised geometry.

How Newton was introduced to the most advanced mathematical texts of his day, including Descartes', is not very clear. But it is accepted that his first interest in the mathematics that governs the universe came in the form of an astrology book that he found in the autumn of 1663 at a fair in Cambridge.

Sir Isaac Newton was a professor at Trinity College, Cambridge University, England.

Isaac Newton's name scratched in a window ledge at Grantham Free School.

THE UNWANTED ORPHAN

Isaac Newton's life can be divided into three quite distinct periods, of which most of us know only the second.

The first period is the one that covers his boyhood days from 1643 up to his appointment as a Cambridge University professor in 1669.

The second period from 1669 to 1687 spans Newton's period as Lucasian professor at Cambridge.

The third period, hardly ever remembered, but nearly as long as the other two combined, sees Newton as a highly paid government official for the National Mint in London, showing little interest in further mathematical research.

Of the first period, it is interesting to note that, following the death of his father, Newton's mother, Hannah Ayscough, married the minister of a church in a nearby village when Isaac was two years old. Left in the care of his grandmother, the young child was more or less treated as an unwanted orphan. There is no doubt that Isaac felt very bitter about his upbringing. When looking back on 'his sins' at age nineteen, Isaac lists:

'*Threatening my father and mother… to burn them and the house over them*'.

It was an uncle, William Ayscough, who gave Isaac his breakthrough, deciding that Isaac should go to university. Under the tutorship of the head teacher of the Grantham Free School, Newton began to learn about the world.

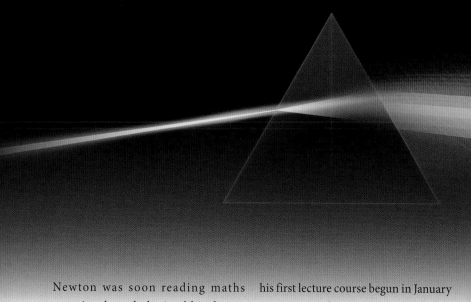

Newton was soon reading maths voraciously and obtained his degree in 1665, the year that the Black Death was rampaging across England. It was because of the plague that Cambridge University was forced later that year to close temporarily, and Isaac had to return to Lincolnshire.

There, in a period of less than two years, while Newton was still under 25 years old, he began revolutionary advances in mathematics, optics, physics, and astronomy.

Newton's first extraordinary discovery was in optics and this was the topic of his first lecture course begun in January 1670. Researching on his own, back in Lincolnshire during the two plague years, he had the insight that white light is not one pure thing, but rather a mixture or composite.

This realization had evaded every thinker since Aristotle, who had taught that white light was a basic single entity. When he passed a thin beam of sunlight through a glass prism, Newton revealed forever the spectrum of colours that was formed.

Of course, Newton's greatest achievement was his work in physics

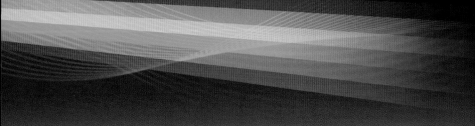

A triangular prism breaks light up into its constituent spectral colours.

and celestial mechanics, which culminated in the theory of universal gravitation. By 1666 Newton had early versions of his three laws of motion. He had also discovered the law giving the centrifugal force on a body moving uniformly in a circular path.

Newton's novel idea of 1666 was to imagine that the Earth's gravity influenced the Moon, counterbalancing its centrifugal force.

It was only in 1687 that the secretive Newton finally published the *Philosophiae Naturalis Principia Mathematica* or *Principia* as it is always known. The *Principia* is recognised as the greatest scientific book ever written. Newton analysed the motion of bodies in resisting and non-resisting media under the action of centripetal forces. The results were applied to orbiting bodies, projectiles, pendulums, and free-fall near the Earth.

He further demonstrated that the planets were attracted toward the Sun by a force varying as the inverse square of the distance and generalised that all heavenly bodies mutually attract one another.

Further generalisation led Newton to the law of universal gravitation:

> *'... all matter attracts all other matter with a force proportional to the product of their masses and inversely proportional to the square of the distance between them.'*

Newton explained a wide range of previously unrelated phenomena: the eccentric orbits of comets, the tides and their variations, the precession of the Earth's axis, and motion of the Moon as perturbed by the gravity of the Sun. This work made Newton an international leader in scientific research. The continental philosophers certainly did not accept the idea of action at a distance. They stubbornly continued to believe in Descartes' vortex theory where forces work through contact.

Given the rage that Newton had shown throughout his life when criticised, it is not surprising that he fell out so spectacularly with Leibniz.

Perhaps all that is worth relating here is that Newton used his position as President of the Royal Society to set up a committee to decide with absolute certainty whether he or Leibniz was the true inventor of calculus.

The official report that was published by the Royal Society, and a review that appeared in the Philosophical Transactions of the Royal Society unambiguously supported his position. This was hardly surprising, really, as Newton was, in fact, the author of all three pieces of work.

Newton, it must be said, was a fanatic. In personal matters, his saying: *'To every action there is always opposed an equal reaction'* did not apply. Newton's reactions to anything were always many times greater.

His assistant, Whiston, had seen his rage at first hand. He wrote:

'Newton was of the most fearful, cautious and suspicious temper that I ever knew.'

Newton's laboratory notebooks are filled not only with details of how he deduced that white light is a mixture of spectral colours, and sober explanations of optical and physical phenomena such as freezing and boiling, but with notes about green lions and dying toads, poisonous dragons and hermaphrodites – the code words used by alchemists.

Close-up of comet C/2011 L4 PANSTARRS as seen from Mount Dale, Western Australia.

his other scientific endeavours.'

John Maynard Keynes, who acquired the world's largest single collection of Newton's alchemical papers, went so far to say that:

Newton dabbled in alchemy as part of his natural research.

'*Newton was not the first of the Age of Reason. He was the last of the magicians.*'

As William Newman says, 'Whatever the ultimate purpose of Newton's alchemical investigations may have been, it is clear that we cannot erect a watertight dam separating them from

Certainly, Newton would not have not called himself a 'scientist', but rather a Natural Philosopher, a philosopher of nature. Such people were rarely, if ever, narrowly associated with a single discipline, as modern scientists invariably are. The leading physicists of the 17th and 18th centuries – the

'Enlightenment' period – were instead philosophers in the broadest sense, people who understood their theoretical and experimental work in the wider context of a world view with religious and political elements included.

Newton is to science what Euclid was to mathematics. Both provided the terms and definitions for all the rest. Newton found it necessary to deal with otherwise apparently philosophical issues, such as those of the nature of 'space' and of 'true motion' (in particular the views of Descartes), in order to address paradoxes such as that of how the Earth could both be 'accelerating' away from the Sun at any moment, and yet be motionless.

If some of his theoretical elements, such as those of 'Absolute Space' let alone 'Absolute Time', seem to have been collapsed by Relativity theory, Einstein was the first to acknowledge that it was Newton who gave the world the framework for investigations.

> *'I do not know what I may appear to the world, but to myself I seem to have been only like a boy playing on the seashore, and diverting myself in now and then finding a smoother pebble or a prettier shell than ordinary, whilst the great ocean of truth lay all undiscovered before me.'*
>
> Isaac Newton

CHAPTER 6
SNIFFING OUT EMPIRICISM WITH LOCKE, BERKELEY AND HUME

'No man's knowledge here can go beyond his experience.'

John Locke

LOCKE'S DOUBLE POLITICAL LEGACY

The scholastic philosophers looked for wisdom and knowledge through introspection and the analysis of words. But the rise of science in the 17th and 18th centuries brought with it a change in the hierarchy of knowledge, and the study of nature again became something much more worthy of philosophers.

Two thousand years earlier, in one of his dialogues, called the *Theaetetus*, Plato had compared everyday sense experience to the process of creating impressions in wax by pressing objects into it.

The object leaves its characteristic impression in the wax, in a similar way that objects around us leave their tell-tale impressions on our minds when we look or hear or smell or taste or touch them. It is this commonsense approach that John Locke expands upon on in the second volume of his *Essays on Human Understanding*.

A wax seal used to authenticate a letter in the 19th century.

Nonetheless, for him, as for Descartes and as for Plato, the mind that assesses or judges things is quite separate from the material objects that create the impressions.

John Locke (1632–1704) was born in a quiet Somerset village into a Puritan trading family, and into a rather less quiet period of the Civil War between Parliament and Royalists.

His political theory, set out in the *Two Treatises on Civil Government* is credited with inspiring both the American and the French Revolutions in the name of fundamental rights and freedoms.

Locke's influence is there in the American Declaration of Independence, in their constitutional separation of powers, and the Bill of Rights.

It is there too in the doctrine of natural rights that appears at the outset of the French Revolution, and in the Declaration of the Rights of Man, 'All being equal and independent, no one ought to harm another in his life, health, liberty, or possessions'.

The drafting committee of the US Declaration of Independence presenting its work to the Congress.

François-Marie Arouet Voltaire.

The French philosopher Voltaire called Locke a man of the greatest wisdom, adding 'What he has not seen clearly, I despair of ever seeing.' A generation later, in America, Locke's reputation had risen still higher. Benjamin Franklin thanked him for his 'self-education'; Thomas Paine spread his radical ideas about revolution and Thomas Jefferson credited him as one of the greatest philosophers of liberty of all time.

But all these star-studded endorsements cannot hide entirely the elephant in Locke's political theory: that civil and political rights are for the haves and not the have-nots.

Locke's *Second Treatise of Civil Government* (published anonymously in 1689) contains a special discussion of slavery. Chapters 4 and 16 give an account of the 'state of slavery'. This explanation in turn depends on his account of the 'state of nature' in Chapter 2 and of the 'state of war', which makes up Chapter 3. In the Second Treatise, Locke offers this vision of a very uncivil society:

Shackles used to restrain slaves – John Locke put forward doubtful arguments to justify slavery.

'...there is another sort of servants, which by a peculiar name we call slaves, who being captives taken in a just war, are by the right of nature subjected to the absolute dominion and arbitrary power of their masters. These men having, as I say, forfeited their lives, and with it their liberties, and lost their estates; and being in the state of slavery, not capable of any property, cannot in that state be considered as any part of civil society; the chief end whereof is the preservation of property.'

DOUBLE STANDARDS

Nowadays philosophers don't talk much about Locke's view of slaves. But that does not mean the subject was an irrelevance. Because in Locke's philosophy, property is the key to 'civil' society, and the key to property is labour.

Indeed, as morality for him starts with the institution of property, slavery is a very peculiar but significant case. In another section of the *Two Treatises*, notwithstanding his other arguments, Locke urges that slavery is 'so vile and miserable an Estate of Man' and 'so directly opposed to the benevolent

Slaves gathering cotton an a plantation in Georgia, USA.

temper and spirit of the nation' that it was 'hardly to be conceived that any Englishman, much less a Gentleman, should plead for it.' The natural liberty of man here represents an inalienable freedom from absolute, arbitrary power. Locke's position on liberty is, let us say, ambiguous. What is unambiguous is that Locke invested personally and substantially in the Royal African Company, one of the cruellest English slave traders.

Referring to his political writings, Bertrand Russell called him the 'apostle' of the English revolution. Locke certainly had a profound influence on the development of Western democracies and political life in Europe and beyond. Yet, even if it is not so often noted, the great success of his political arguments rests at least in part on the success of his metaphysical ones.

Locke held major investments in a slave trading company.

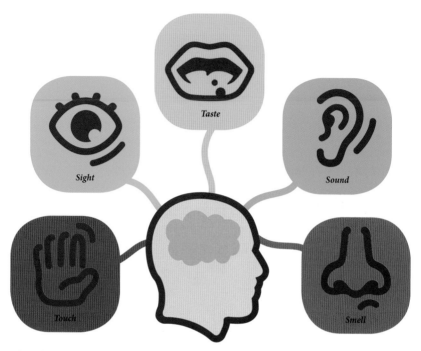

John Locke argued that the mind made sense of its surroundings using the information transmitted to it by the senses.

Chief among Locke's metaphysical arguments is his theory that the human mind creates its view of the world out of the raw data that it receives via the senses. This idea is the core of the philosophical doctrine that is now known as Empiricism.

Tall and thin, with a long nose like a horse, and what one biographer has called 'soft, melancholy eyes', Locke had the good fortune of fitting his times. His views on how the mind works were seen as just the antidote everyone was looking for to Descartes' dualism.

AN ESSAY CONCERNING HUMAN UNDERSTANDING

'All ideas come from sensation or reflection. Let us then suppose the mind to be, as we say, a blank tablet (tabula rasa), void of all characters without any ideas; how comes it to be furnished?

'Whence comes it by that vast store, which the busy and boundless fancy of man has painted on it with an almost endless variety? Whence has it all the materials of reason and knowledge? To this I answer, in one word, from experience: in that all our knowledge is founded, and from that it ultimately derives itself.

'Our observation, employed either about external sensible objects, or about the internal operations of our minds, perceived and reflected on by ourselves is that which supplies our understandings with all the materials of thinking.

'These two are the fountains of knowledge, from whence all the ideas we have, or can naturally have, do spring.'

Locke said our experiences – information supplied by our senses – are the source of our knowledge.

*Locke was influenced by the
Irish scientist Robert Boyle.*

In describing how the mind might take in 'simple or complex ideas' via the senses, before assembling them to create knowledge, Locke perfectly reflected the mechanistic science of the time.

Of Locke's two most immediate philosophical followers, George Berkeley and David Hume – the first an Irish bishop and the second a Scottish agnostic – neither thinker has had anything like the same practical impact on the world.

Berkeley, despite being in many ways a dedicated and principled servant of the ordinary people, produced a theory that seemed to many then and since to be merely ridiculous, while Hume, for all his many good points, was essentially a political reactionary who disowned his own philosophy as hopelessly impractical.

The title of Locke's essay, *On Human Understanding*, is rather bland, but it is really about the way the human mind gathers, organises and makes sense of data about the world.

Putting it that way makes it sound quite scientific in style, and Locke indeed knew and was influenced by two great contemporary scientists of the time – Robert Boyle and Isaac Newton.

Newton was notoriously solitary and secretive and had little time for most people, jealously protecting his ideas, but he counted Locke as a valuable, respected contact.

John Locke knew and followed the work of Isaac Newton.

PRIMARIES AND SECONDARIES

Let's look at Locke's theory of perception. It is very much a cross-over theory between the old way of doing philosophy and the new scientific approaches to knowledge.

Locke's approach here is rooted in a rather dubious distinction between so-called primary and secondary qualities. The primary qualities are supposed to be somehow inseparable from the actual 'thing', whatever it may be, and are specified as: solidity, extensions, figure, motion and quantity or number.

Motion was integral to Locke's theory of perception.

REAL AND UNREAL QUALITIES

Locke distinguishes between what he calls the primary qualities of objects, and their secondary ones. The crucial distinction is that the first kind of quality is 'really there' in the object, but the secondary quality is only produced in our mind as we perceive the object using our senses.

Locke argued that we could combine our impressions of other things to imagine what, for example, a winged horse would look like.

The idea is that if a tree fell in the forest, the result would be movements of air molecules – a primary quality. To speak of say, the 'sound' of it falling means nothing if there was no one and nothing there to 'hear' it.

Locke splits ideas into simple and complex: simple ideas are the immediate result of sense perception, like the sensation of 'yellow' when we look at a banana.

Complex ideas, on the other hand, must be constructed out of simple ideas with a little mental processing. The second part of his project is to explain how the sophistication that the mind is capable of could arise.

His simple explanation is that we do not need to ever to see a winged horse to know what it looks like. Our brain can construct the idea of one using previous experiences of seeing ordinary horses and winged animals like birds.

Movement, sound and colour
were all examined by Locke.

The secondary qualities, easier to grasp, are things like colour, smell and sound. Locke points some of the ways by which secondary qualities are easily mistaken, but Berkeley was only stating the obvious when he responded that primary qualities are also often the subject of errors.

Locke's distinctions were adopted by the new philosophers of nature, who reinterpreted the world in terms of solids moving with particular velocities and in the process creating impressions and sensations in human onlookers.

Sounds, for example, became the effect produced when vibrating air molecules

cause further vibrations in the ear, to produce an effect in the mind.

Locke's approach to all such questions, influenced by Descartes, was first of all to consider what things we know with certainty, or as a lawyer might put it, more carefully, with 'reasonable certainty', along with a second stage of propositions which it is useful to accept in practice, even though they may appear less than totally certain.

'The grounds of probability are two: conformity with our own experience, or the testimony of others' experience,' writes Locke, thus setting a pretty low bar.

After all, as Bertrand Russell quips, the King of Siam ceased to believe what Europeans told him about science and philosophy when they started to describe ice and snow.

However, Locke is refreshingly undogmatic in his approach, writing:

'How can we expect, I say, that opinions thus settled should be given up to the arguments or authority of a stranger or adversary, especially if there be any suspicion of interest or design, as there never fails to be, where men find themselves ill treated?

Snow and ice were beyond the imagination of the King of Siam.

We should do well to commiserate our mutual ignorance, and endeavour to remove it in all the gentle and fair ways of information; and not instantly treat others ill, as obstinate and perverse, because they will not renounce their own, and receive our opinions, or at least those we would force upon them, when it is more than probable that we are no less obstinate in not embracing some of theirs.'

An Essay Concerning Human Understanding

WHAT ARE IDEAS?

The mind, at birth, is a blank sheet, upon which experience writes its beautiful stories. In Locke's time, this sort of claim was not only novel, but politically radical.

Locke is similarly briskly disinterested in metaphysics about which (writing to a friend about Leibniz's latest theory) he supposes 'you and I have had enough of this kind of fiddling.'

His approach is essentially that of a careful technician; he does not see himself as a grand theorist at all.

The doctrine of empiricism fits very well into this mindset. At its heart is the idea that knowledge is merely pieced together out of everyday humdrum experiences. Since we can only think in terms of ideas, and since all ideas are created from previous sense perceptions, it follows, Locke says, that all our ideas come from sense perception, too.

For centuries, the scholastic philosophers (following the Ancients) had built their systems from the contrary assumption that the human mind had some kind of built-in access to all the important truths.

Plato carefully argues against the idea that sense perception is the source of 'real knowledge', believing it instead to be the problem – the source of error.

There are other problems for the

Locke argued that all of our ideas start with our senses.

idea that knowledge is limited to that which we have previously experienced, even if it is supposed that the mind can be aware of things that on the face of it have not been and cannot be experienced – perhaps by merging two properties creatively Locke considers this 'partial solution' but evidently finds it unconvincing. In places, he seems to offer a quite different theory in which knowledge is recast in such a way that there are new categories of knowledge possible.

There is intuitive knowledge (which covers things like the awareness of our own consciousness and existence) and 'demonstrative' knowledge, which includes knowledge of things like mathematical relationships and the existence of God.

$$\frac{x+1}{x+2} - \frac{x+2}{x+3}$$

$$\frac{7x-5}{2x^2-3x+1} - \frac{7x+}{1-x-}$$

$$\frac{4}{x+3} - \frac{x+2}{x}$$

Demonstrative knowledge like mathematics was, according to Locke, different from intuitive knowledge.

Scottish historian, diplomat and philosopher, David Hume.

Another problem in all of this is that Locke assumes that sense experience, meaning the internal mental sensations created by 'who knows what' outside, correspond in some direct and consistent way. But he has, of course, no way of proving this.

As Descartes warns, in many ways sensations can be treacherous messengers. In empiricism, we know only the experiences, never the causes.

There's no easy answer to this. David Hume more-or-less proved later that sensations do not have any logical link to any underlying reality, while Bishop Berkeley maintains that there is really no need to create the extra theoretical layer in any case.

The debate can be reconstructed as a dispute about the relation between 'mind and matter'. Descartes split the two apart, and Locke reconnects them in a very nice, tidy way – but creates a paradox in so doing. Matter, it seems, even today, is supposed to be imaginary: a table is colourless and it was soon realised that those primary qualities of solidity, dimensions and so on are illusory too, melting away under the microscope.

But minds are not so simple either – they appear to require both streams of impressions (as well as holding past sensations in the memory) along with systems for making sense of the vast mass of information. Take away sensation, take away memory, what is left for mind?

Bishop George Berkeley has a rather dramatic answer to that question.

Berkeley (1685–1753) is a very subtle thinker. He takes on the materialism of Locke and Newton and applies logical rigour to it. He insists that objects actually don't really exist, and instead our impressions are real.

An 18th-century etching of Bishop George Berkeley.

According to Bishop Berkeley, seeing a tree does not mean the tree you are seeing is exactly as you see it.

WITTY DIALOGUES

The conventional view supposes that there are objects out there that have an effect on us which produces impressions in our minds. Berkeley points out that what we 'see' in our heads – be it as a memory of the tree, or a dream of the tree, or an actual observation of the tree – is never the actual thing.

Accordingly, it is always a matter of conjecture to suppose that there is a direct link between the image in our mind and the 'thing itself out there'.

It is through a series of witty dialogues that Berkeley argues for the position that we have access only to these mental phenomena: to ideas.

Locke had accepted that this gap existed for what he called the 'secondary qualities' (colours, smells, tastes) but Berkeley argues firmly that it is simply not possible to draw a substantial distinction between the primary and the secondary qualities.

What is sauce for the goose, is sauce for the gander. The human mind perceives nothing other than its internally created images of reality. Put another way, everything is mind-dependent.

'Berkeley is a most striking and even unique phenomenon in the history of philosophy,' declares Geoffrey Warnock, in a book entitled *The Great Philosophers*, although, alas, he never pins down exactly what he thought was striking or 'even unique' about him.

Was it that Berkeley published his grand metaphysical theory at a precociously early age? Was it because he presented most of his philosophy pithily and wittily in the style (forever associated with Plato) of little dialogues?

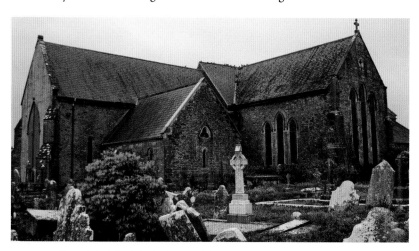

Cloyne Cathedral in Ireland – George Berkeley was appointed Bishop of Cloyne in 1734.

In actual fact, Bishop Berkeley might be considered an oddity amongst philosophers just because he had a social conscience and campaigned actively for the poor people of his native Ireland, suffering as ever at the hands of those two pestilential forces: famine and English settlers.

And there is another candidate reason for Berkeley being considered a philosophical curiosity: he was the first major European philosopher to visit America. It was in America that he tried and, in due course, failed to set up a college to save the souls of the unfortunate slaves and Indians of the Caribbean and south eastern coast of America. In the process, he discovered a miracle cure made from the sap of pine trees.

Just as with his theory about ideas, the physical mechanism for the cure was unknown and, to Berkeley, uninteresting too. For all Berkeley cared, the cure worked directly on the mind.

Whitehall Museum House on Rhode Island in the US, built by George Berkeley in the 18th century.

A MIRACLE CURE

Berkeley recommended that tar-water be prepared by pouring a gallon of water over a quart of the sap of pine trees, then stirring thoroughly with a ladle or flat stick. After being allowed to stand for 48 hours to let the tar settle, the clear layer was poured off and kept for use. Berkeley believed that a pint of tar-water a day would cure almost every disease then known.

The use of the medicine is mentioned in Charles Dickens's *Great Expectations*. Young Pip and his brother-in-law, Joe, were forced to take the 'foul tasting' medicine whether they were ill or not, as sort of cruel health ritual!

'Some medical beast had revived tar-water in those days as a fine medicine, and Mrs. Joe always kept a supply of it in the cupboard; having a belief in its virtues correspondent to its nastiness.

At the best of times, so much of this elixir was administered to me as a choice restorative, that I was conscious of going about, smelling like a new fence.'

Charles Dickens:
Great Expectations

Charles Dickens was not a fan of
Bishop Berkeley's cure-all.

SCEPTICAL THINKING

In place of the mathematically tidy and predictable world of Newton and Locke, Berkeley offers up a kind of 'radical immaterialism' in which the world loses its objective reality.

Instead, the world becomes intricately connected with whoever happens to be looking at it. '*Esse est percipi*', or 'to be, is to be perceived.'

One company's version of Berkeley's 'Tar Water' cure for coughs and colds contained alcohol, morphia, tartaric acid and chloroform!

Berkeley's theory, however, was out of touch with the times. There was much more contemporary interest in his miraculous 'Tar Water' cure and his plan to create a 'University for Indians' in the New World than there was in his philosophical ideas. Berkeley had previously helped to establish a home and school for orphan children near where he lived in London and the 'Bermuda College' university idea was even discussed in the British Parliament and received Royal approval.

So it falls to David Hume (1711–1776) to settle the issue raised by Locke and challenged by Berkeley. If Hume seems to start out like Locke by being sensible and empirical, he ends up at a very different place.

Where Locke appeals to common sense, Hume finds experience proves to be a totally inadequate guide to knowledge, and that the only rational thing is to jettison all that it offers. He writes, in characteristic style, that in all the incidents of life we ought still to preserve our scepticism.

'If we believe, that fire warms, or water refreshes, it is only because it costs us too much pains to think otherwise. Nay if we are philosophers, it ought only to be upon sceptical principles, and from an inclination, which we feel to the employing ourselves after that manner. Where reason is lively, and mixes itself with some propensity, it ought to be assented to. Where it does not, it never can have any title to operate upon us.'

Statue of David Hume in Edinburgh, Scotland.

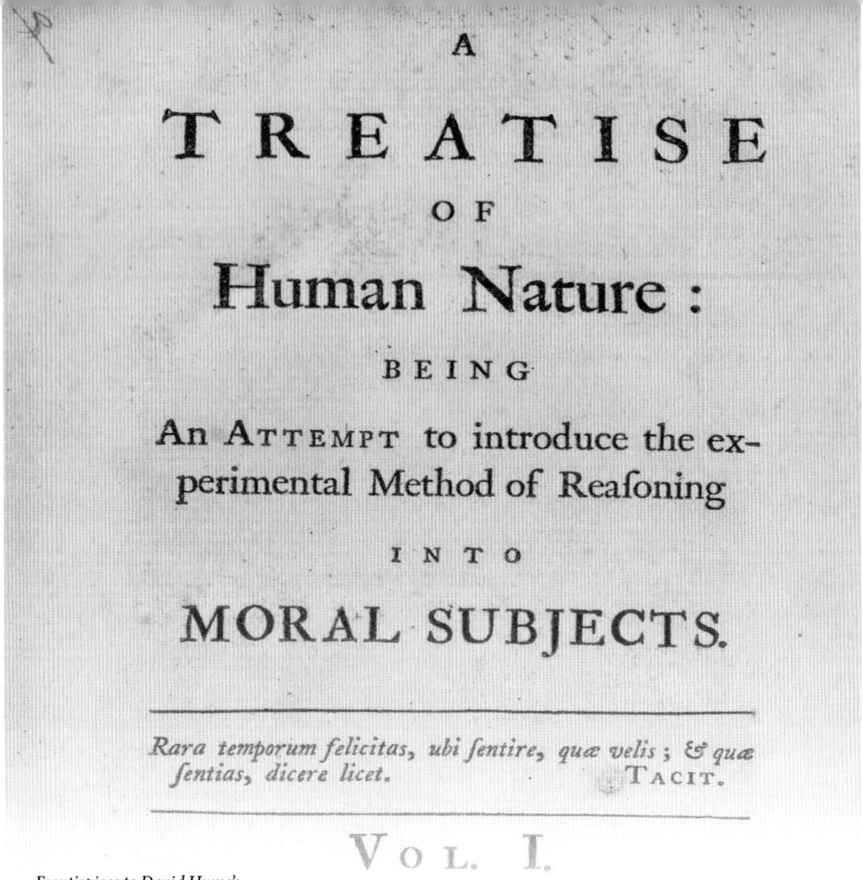

A

TREATISE

OF

Human Nature :

BEING

An ATTEMPT to introduce the experimental Method of Reasoning

INTO

MORAL SUBJECTS.

Rara temporum felicitas, ubi sentire, quæ velis ; & quæ sentias, dicere licet. TACIT.

VOL. I.

Frontispiece to David Hume's Treatise of Human Nature.

Hume comes quickly to the conclusion that there is, in fact, no such thing as a truly rational belief.

From Locke, Hume takes further the idea that human knowledge is essentially created out of the relations of ideas, with the ideas themselves rooted in sense impressions. First, anything not rooted in sense impression, Hume throws out as mere nonsense.

Hume studied at Edinburgh University but was denied a post there due to his atheism.

'At the time, therefore, that I am tired with amusement and company, and have indulged a reverie in my chamber, or in a solitary walk by a river-side, I feel my mind all collected within itself, and am naturally inclined to carry my view into all those subjects, about which I have met with so many disputes in the course of my reading and conversation.

'I cannot forbear having a curiosity to be acquainted with the principles of moral good and evil, the nature and foundation of government, and the cause of those several passions and inclinations, which actuate and govern me. I am uneasy to think I approve of one object, and disapprove of another; call one thing beautiful, and another deformed; decide concerning truth and falsehood, reason and folly, without knowing upon what principles I proceed.

'I am concerned for the condition of the learned world, which lies under such deplorable ignorance in all these particulars. I feel an ambition to arise in me of contributing to the instruction of mankind, and of acquiring a name by my inventions and discoveries. These sentiments spring up naturally in my present disposition; and should I endeavour to banish them, by attaching myself to any other business or diversion, I feel I should be a loser in point of pleasure; and this is the origin of my philosophy.'

A Treatise of Human Nature (Concluding section)

Out goes the notion of God (or gods), the human soul, or even the psychological inner self, and various key concepts we use to structure the world, which are not actually possible to explain from within it. These include things like cause and effect, the assumption that the rules governing the future will be like those that governed the past, and the principle of drawing conclusions from limited amounts of evidence, for example.

'If we take in our hand any volume; of divinity or school metaphysics, for instance; let us ask, Does it contain any abstract reasoning concerning quantity or number? No. Does it contain any experimental reasoning concerning matter of fact and existence? No. Commit it then to the flames: for it can contain nothing but sophistry and illusion.'

An Enquiry Concerning
Human Understanding

David Hume's home city of Edinburgh, Scotland, at dusk.

Hume similarly rejects the idea that humans and animals are importantly different, saying instead that animals and humans share remarkably similar capacities and use similar methods for solving problems, but humans have superior language skills.

Hume says that many of our reassuring everyday notions are merely lazy conventions. His favourite example is our belief that the sun will rise tomorrow. Clearly, this is well based on many past observations, but (logically speaking) any claim that it will continue to rise tomorrow

cannot be justified by reference to the past. So there is no rational basis for believing that the sun will rise tomorrow. Yet, we do believe it!

In fact, all assumptions about the future based on past experience suppose that the future will always resemble the past, and yet, no such certainty exists.

Many other assumptions are based on habit, not reason, and, ultimately, all assumptions about matters of fact are based in probability. When two events occur together repeatedly, we create a mental link between the two events – a practical rather than a logical tool for dealing with the world.

IMPRESSIONS AND IDEAS

Hume says that there are two kinds of sense experience: impressions and ideas. Impressions are more direct, and have a greater immediacy. Ideas are indeed just the faint smudges left behind by the impressions.

'By ideas,' explains Hume, 'I mean the faint images of these in thinking and reasoning.'

A simple impression, say of an apple, has its own simple idea – an apple. Impressions predate ideas, Hume says firmly. Someone born blind has no concept of colours.

As to your innermost self, your psychological essence (the thing Descartes clings to as a rock), Hume says that there is no way to get an 'impression' of your self. You can search for it as hard as you like, perhaps in the mirror, perhaps in your dreams, but he says you can never actually have any sense in experience of your essential self.

He consigns the concept to the waste basket, writing:

'For my part, when I enter most intimately into what I call myself, I always stumble on some particular perception or other, of heat or cold, light or shade, love or hatred, pain or pleasure. I never can catch myself at any time without a perception, and never can observe any thing but the perception...

'If any one, upon serious and unprejudiced reflection thinks he has a different notion of himself, I must confess I can reason no longer with him.

'All I can allow him is, that he may be in the right as well as I, and that we are essentially different in this particular. He may, perhaps, perceive something simple and continued, which he calls himself; tho' I am certain there is no such principle in me.'

A Treatise of Human Nature

*Hume claimed that you can never
actually experience your essential self.*

When Hume dismisses the possibility of there being any individual 'self', he also, of course, destroys the Christian idea of the soul.

Hume's attack is part of a more general one in which he rejects the simplistic division of the world into subject and object: the consciousness is not exactly an object, and not exactly a subject. But in saying that, therefore, it does not exist, seems a step he is not really entitled to take.

As far as physical science goes, Hume is nowadays considered to be entirely correct. X does not cause Y, whatever simple folk may imagine. It is rather – as Hume puts it – our lazy ways of thinking, our ways born of old habit, that lead us to connect two things that are logically forever distinct.

Hume delved into the human mind to study consciousness and our ways of thinking.

HOW THE HUMAN MIND INVENTS THE WORLD

Hume's sweeping scepticism takes on no less that seven key philosophical relationships.

As well as personal identity, there are:

resemblance

relations of time and space

relations of quantity and number

degrees of quality or kind

causation

Hume considered all the everyday relationships of time, space and causation to be philosophically suspect.

'For as all our reasonings concerning existence are derived from causation, and as all our reasonings concerning causation are derived from the experienced conjunction of objects, not from any reasoning or reflection, the same experience must give us a notion of these objects, and must remove all mystery from our conclusions. This is so evident, that it would scarce have merited our attention, were it not to obviate certain objections of this kind, which might arise against the following reasonings concerning matter and substance. I need not observe, that a full knowledge of the object is not requisite, but only of those qualities of it, which we believe to exist.'

A Treatise of Human Nature

LOOMING DOUBT

David Hume's casual, lazy style, as much as his plump and expressionless face, belies a cunning and determination that Rousseau once described as, quite simply, terrifying.

Religion has no place and no role in Hume's philosophy. Knowledge, ethics and God are all obliged to return to Earth for Hume's scrutiny.

Portal of the former Jesuit College Henri IV in La Flèche (Sarthe), where Hume debated religion with the Jesuits.

In all this, as Bertrand Russell says, 'he hoped for vehement attacks, which he would meet with brilliant retorts.'

Yet the *Treatise* fell, famously, 'dead-born' from the press. Later revisions of it, the two 'Enquiries', the first *Concerning Human Understanding* (1748) and the other *Concerning the Principles of Morals* (1751) also failed to receive the attention that he thought they really deserved.

But then, Hume's philosophy, as Bertrand Russell also observed, is a dead-end. 'In his direction it is impossible to go further.'

Hume drafted his book while staying in La Flèche, the small French town that Descartes himself had lived in, and fittingly introduces his book by announcing that there are only the two kinds of genuine knowledge: that born from experience and experiment, and that born from rationally examining relationships. The rest of it needs to be doubted.

Later, introducing a new version of his ideas, Hume explained his aims more generally as to enquire whether anything 'can be ascertained in philosophy.'

It is, he says, not merely 'the same system of doubt as that of Robert Boyle and others' which 'merely went to show the uncertainty of the conclusions attending particular species of argument' but 'a sweeping argument to show that by the structure of the understanding, the result of all investigations, on all subjects, must ever be doubt.'

View of the Loire Bridge in front of the Town Hall at La Flèche.

Hume saw himself as distinctly different from everyone around him.

THE LONELY MAN

'My intention then in displaying so carefully the arguments of that fantastic sect [the philosophical sceptics], *is only to make the reader sensible of the truth of my hypothesis, that all our reasonings concerning causes and effects are derived from nothing but custom; and that belief is more properly an act of the, sensitive, than of the cogitative part of our natures.'*

A Treatise of Human Nature

In a very distinctive passage, reminiscent of the *Meditations*, where Descartes warns of the effects of jettisoning even temporarily all his conventional assumptions, Hume speaks of his restless philosophy, and of the feelings it produces in his mind.

'I am first affrighted and confounded with that forlorn solitude in which I am placed in my philosophy, and fancy myself some strange uncouth monster, who, not being able to mingle and unite in society, has been expelled all human commerce, and left utterly abandoned and disconsolate.

'Fain would I run into the crowd for shelter and warmth, but cannot prevail with myself to mix with such deformity. I call upon others to join me, in order to make a company apart, but no one will hearken to me. Every one keeps at a distance, and dreads that storm which beats upon me from every side.

'I have exposed myself to the enmity of all metaphysicians, logicians, mathematicians, and even theologians; and can I wonder at the insults I must suffer? I have declared my disapprobation of their systems; and can I be surprised if they should express a hatred of mine and of my person?

'When I look abroad, I foresee on every side dispute, contradiction, anger, calumny, and detraction.

'When I turn my eye inward, I find nothing but doubt and ignorance. All the world conspires to oppose and contradict me: though such is my weakness, that I feel all my opinions loosen and fall of themselves, when unsupported by the approbation of others.

'Every step I take is with hesitation, and every new reflection makes me dread an error and absurdity in my reasoning.'

It was not until 1756 that his opponents organised themselves enough to present a summary of the Treatise to the Edinburgh Church court. They believed that Hume should be tried for heresy.

A close reading of his writings showed, they said, that Hume believed:

'First, that all distinction between virtue and vice is merely imaginary.

'Second, that justice has no foundation farther than it contributes to public advantage.

'Third, that adultery is very lawful, but sometimes not expedient

'Fourth, that religion and its ministers are prejudicial to mankind, and will always be found either to run into the heights of superstition or enthusiasm.

'Fifth, that Christianity has no evidence of its being a divine revelation.

'Sixth, that of all the modes of Christianity, popery is the best, and the reformation from thence was only the work of madmen and enthusiasts.'

Their wrath was all the greater because Hume was actually less of a disbeliever than a deviant believer, an agnostic more than an atheist.

Years later, Hume declared at one of his beloved soirées in Paris that he had never met an atheist and questioned whether they really existed. His host, the Baron D'Holbach, replied firmly that he was dining with seventeen of them!

There were calls for Hume to be tried for heresy due to his criticism of Christianity.

Anyway, and alas, given Hume's thirst for literary controversy, the Church at the time had had enough of such trials, and the authorities declined to pursue 'so abstruse and metaphysical a subject', ruling that it 'would be more for the purposes of edification to dismiss the process.'

John Stuart Mill, writing a history review some time after Hume had departed this Earth and could no longer be offended, commented favourably on Hume's intellect, but deplored his honesty, saying that:

'He reasoned with surprising acuteness; but the object of his reasoning was not to obtain truth, but to show that it is unattainable. His mind too was completely enslaved by a taste for literature; not those kinds of literature which teach mankind to know the causes of their happiness and misery, that they may seek the one and avoid the other; but that literature which without regard for truth or utility, seeks only to excite emotion.'

The Palace of Versailles, Paris, France – Hume spent his happiest years in Paris as a British diplomat.

*English philosopher
John Stuart Mill.*

HIS OWN WORDS

Perhaps the final word on Hume should go to himself. Unlike most philosophers, Hume took the opportunity (albeit the rather late one offered by being confined to his deathbed) to write his own autobiography.

Autobiography may be the wrong word. It was more an attempt to dictate the terms by which posterity would record, interpret and understand him. One commentator called it 'that curious memoir', which Hume entitled:

THE LIFE OF DAVID HUME, ESQ. WRITTEN BY HIMSELF.

Augustine had pioneered the genre, with his Confessions, but this is no confessional account, it is rather a catalogue of Hume's achievements. It starts with a brief sketch of his youth in which he remarks:

'I passed through the ordinary course of education with success, and was seized very early with a passion for literature, which has been the ruling passion of my life, and the great source of my enjoyments...

Shortly after this, Hume says, that he settled upon 'that plan of life which I have steadily and successfully pursued. I resolved to make a very rigid frugality supply my deficiency of fortune, to maintain unimpaired my independency, and to regard every object as contemptible, except the improvement of my talents in literature.'

Hume, like Plato, is not a philosopher wracked by logical doubts, but rather a writer who enjoys a good yarn. But he left his fellow philosophers with many new questions to answer.

Books and literature were Hume's passion.

Image of St Augustine in Cologne Cathedral, Germany.

CHAPTER 7
CAPITALISM AND THE RATIONAL MAN

'Labour is the source of all wealth, the political economists assert. And it really is the source – next to nature, which supplies it with the material that it converts into wealth. But it is even infinitely more than this. It is the prime basic condition for all human existence, and this to such an extent that, in a sense, we have to say that labour created man himself.'

Friedrich Engels
The Part Played by Labour in The Transition from Ape to Man (1876)

Friedrich Engels.

AN ORDERLY MIND

Kant is a philosophers' philosopher. Everything to his mind can be explained and put in its proper place – if only you are logical and rigorous enough.

He practised what he preached, too, rising at exactly the same time each day, eating precisely calculated meals, taking just the appropriate amount of time off for a walk, and afterwards writing voluminously on all subjects under the sun. Kant is celebrated for his essays on ethics and reasoning, but he also made important contributions in many other fields, including astronomy and maths.

Kant was born and lived all his life in the town of Königsberg, then culturally German but today, as Kaliningrad, a Russian exclave between Poland and Lithuania. His childhood was dominated by Protestant religious virtues.

At school, he was given a hefty dose of theology and the classics, being, apparently, particularly taken by the grand metaphysical poetry of Lucretius.

German philosopher Immanuel Kant.

Immanuel Kant's statue in Kaliningrad, now a Russian enclave.

'Ergo vivida vis pervicet et extra
    processit longe flamentia moenia
    mundi atque omne immensum
    peragravit mente animoque.'

'The vivid force of his mind
    prevailed, and he fared forth far
    beyond the flaming ramparts of the
    heavens and traversed the boundless
    universe in thought and mind.'

Lucretius
De Rerum Natura
('On the Nature of Things')
Book I, line 72.

Later, as a professor, he taught an impressive range of subjects: mathematics, anthropology, natural sciences, geography, logic, philosophy, theology, even construction and pyrotechnics. In those days, a professor did not receive a salary and was paid directly by the customers – the students who came to a lecture.

The ancient Greek Muses dictated key aspects of Kant's social life.

Kant's philosophical search for rules started with many odd personal habits. He enjoyed regular meals with a number of intellectual friends but this number was always at least three, the number of Classical Graces, and could never be more than nine, the number of the Ancient Greek Muses.

The conversation at Kant's table spanned a broad range of topics, and Kant always showed a keen interest in the latest political, economic and scientific developments. He was known for his wit and his memory for detail, so that he could describe in detail a foreign town, despite never having visited it.

Kant's early work is characterised by an attempt to identify internal contradictions in abstract metaphysical theories derived from pure logic. For example, Kant is concerned that although in logic either A or not-A is true, in reality, something can be both A and not-A. A physical object like a table on a train, for instance, can be both in motion and motionless since it depends on the position of the observer.

In similar spirit, he also examines the nature of causality and the proofs for the existence of God. At this point in his philosophy, Kant takes on board some of the scepticism that originates in British Empiricism (in particular Hume), but is still very much anchored in the metaphysical tradition.

And then comes the 'Critical Turn'. This is where Kant makes what he describes as the 'revolutionary' move of suggesting that, since there has been little success in attempting to account for knowledge as conforming to the objects of our experience, it is a more promising approach to consider these objects as having to conform to our cognitive faculties.

A table on a train appears motionless to those on the train, but moving to those who are not.

KANT OFFENDS THE CHURCH

In a book called *Religion within the Bounds of Bare Reason*, (1793) Kant tries (as the title suggests) to put religious belief on a sound, logical footing.

One argument offered is that since (alas) happiness is not fully achievable in the empirical world, it is rational to suppose that there must be a mechanism of sorts for achieving it elsewhere. Kant suggests that the there must be immortal souls that are able to work towards the goal.

At the same time, in order to emphasise the primacy of a religion centred around morality, he distances himself from the institutional and ritualistic aspects of religion . He even suggests that religion ought not require more of people than that they behave morally, a suggestion which, in principle, threatened to undercut the status and powers of the church authorities in his time.

So Kant, despite being in many ways a very timid figure, became involved in a political controversy with the Prussian Protestant church. The church pressured Friedrich-Wilhelm II to make Kant agree to abstain from further expressing his opinions on the subject of religion.

Königsberg Cathedral in Kant's home of Kaliningrad.

Kant tried to resolve the debate between the rationalists and the empiricists.

The Turn was marked by the publication of his three *Critiques*. The first is on Pure Reason, the second on Practical Reason and the third, which is less often mentioned, is 'of Judgement'.

In the first, Kant tries to settle the debate created by the tug-of-war between the rationalists (like Descartes) who sought to make sense of the universe through abstract reasoning, and the empiricists (like Locke and Hume) who insisted that knowledge can only come from sense perception and practical observation.

Kant's aim is to combine the two approaches. The key to doing this is to ask what preconditions are required for any experiences of the world anyway?

Kant believed that the human mind has built-in structures for dealing with thoughts and information.

Kant assumes that before the human mind can perceive, it must already have in place some kind of theoretical, methodological framework to make sense of otherwise meaningless data.

In other words, the mind comes with built-in structures that impose regularity on the world that would not otherwise be there. He offers certain categories to illustrate this, setting them out in tables of opposites.

There is for example, an opposition between 'quality' which can be either affirmative, negative or infinite, and 'relation', which can be categorical, hypothetical and disjunctive.

Don't worry if you can't make much sense of that – you're in good company, – and I think it's fair to say that Kant's reputation rests in large part on his perplexing obscurity.

Indeed, one translator (who is in

other senses an admirer) says of Kant that, 'He wearies by frequent repetition, and employs a great number of words to express, in the clumsiest way, what could have been enounced more clearly and distinctly with a few.'

The various (obscure) distinctions that he makes are then placed in a spatial and temporal framework.

Thus, the categories of space and time, which he calls 'forms of intuition', are imposed on sense experience (on 'phenomena') by the human mind in order that the mind can then make sense of it all.

This point had been stressed by Berkeley earlier, so it was not an entirely new concept, but Kant was enormously proud of his originality and grandly compared his insight to the way that Copernicus had upturned the entire Solar System.

MIND GAMES

Kant's own Copernican Revolution was to make the human mind active in organizing the world, where both rationalists and empiricists had left it passive.

The rationalists did so by supposing that the mind came with built-in templates, and the empiricists by supposing that it is a blank slate that responds to outside stimuli.

Kant says that it is through the creation of abstract principles that the mind imposes order upon experience and generates knowledge.

The categories are necessary for self-consciousness, or 'apperception', as Kant calls it, using a Leibnizian term.

The parallel task for the *Critique of Practical Reason*, however, is to put ethics on a rational basis.

This time, Kant comes up with a general rule which he calls the 'categorical imperative'. He offers several different formulations but it is usually expressed as:

'Act only according to that maxim whereby you can at the same time will that it should become a universal law without contradiction.'

Kant is honoured with a bust in the Walhalla Hall of Fame, in Donaustauf, Germany.

KANT'S TASTE FOR RIDDLES

A large part of his most celebrated publication, *The Critique of Pure Reason*, is devoted to exposing the errors that result from misunderstanding the true nature of space and time.

The first paradox he offers is that the universe must have had a beginning in both time and space – and that it cannot have done.

The second is that everything must be made up of ever smaller parts – and that ultimately everything must be made up of the same thing.

The third is that cause and effect are an entirely mechanical, physical phenomenon – and that cause and effect are not a physical phenomenon at all.

Lastly, he says, riddlingly, if God exists, then He must do so as a matter of logic – and yet, logically, God does not need to exist.

Treating others as you would have them treat you is not always an infallible rule for the moral life.

Again, Kant thought this a highly original breakthrough, but the axiom is very like the old injunction (known as the Golden Rule) to treat others only as you would like them to treat you. This is very good advice but often falls down in practice.

For example, suppose someone (perhaps a monk) likes to be cold and hungry and sleep on the floor, as they imagine that this is a virtuous way to live.

For them the rule implies that they would make their children likewise cold and hungry and sleep on the floor, and indeed as many other people as they can. But why is their action virtuous? The children may not wish to be like this.

Or consider the problem of the mad knifeman, which Plato raises in one of his little playlets. If a madman knocks at the door in a bad temper and asks you to return the knife you borrowed the week before, as he has some matter he wants to settle with his neighbour, then Kant would say that you should return it, as the institution of lending requires it. No exceptions!

Similarly, having returned the knife, you can't lie to the mad knifeman about where the neighbour is hiding under the bed as lying is (for Kant) always wrong.

Such simplicities are typical of Kant, but his status is high in the philosophical firmament nonetheless. Representing the conventional view, Philip Stokes, who is a shrewd judge in many ways, calls him 'probably the greatest and

Plato's mad knifeman posed a problem for Kant.

most influential philosopher since Aristotle.'

Russell, however, is less effusive. Referring to the issue of cause and effect, he says that if Kant claimed that he was 'awakened from his dogmatic slumbers' by Hume's criticism of the concept of cause and effect, the awakening was only temporary, as he clearly 'soon invented a soporific which enabled him to sleep again.'

Russell's unkind assessment of Kant seems to be amply borne out by Kant's own words, when he writes:

> 'My investigations led me to the conclusion that the objects with which we are familiar are by no means things in themselves, but are simply phenomena, connected in a certain way with experience. So that without contradiction they cannot be separated from that connection.
>
> 'Only by that experience can they be recognised. I was able to prove the objective reality of the concept of cause in regard to objects of experience, and to demonstrate its origin from pure understanding, without experimental or empirical sources. Thus, I first destroyed the source of scepticism, and then the resulting scepticism itself.'

The Critique of Practical Reason

What was Kant's brilliant solution that had evaded Hume? It was (he thought) to create a distinction between the world we perceive, that is created by our mental categories and that he calls the 'phenomenal' one, and the 'underlying world', with which we cannot directly engage, that he calls the 'noumenal' one.

A side-effect of the solution, which Kant thought was acceptable, is that humans are forever estranged from the fundamental reality. However, Georg Wilhelm Friedrich Hegel, another German-language philosopher, and overlapping in lifetimes, found this restriction quite intolerable. and devoted his philosophical efforts precisely to the task of revealing this underlying reality, and throwing light on the noumenal world.

German philosopher Georg Wilhelm Friedrich Hegel.

LIFE OF HEGEL

Georg Wilhelm Friedrich Hegel (1770-1831) was born in Stuttgart into a traditional, conservative family headed by Georg Hegel senior, a minor civil servant.

He was sent to the Tübingen seminary, to be educated alongside the future epic poet, Friedrich Hölderlin, and fellow philosopher Friedrich Schelling. Thus it was that the three of them would together watch the unfolding of the French Revolution and the subsequent rise of Napoleon Bonaparte.

Hegel worked for a time as both a teacher and a newspaper editor.

Indeed, Hegel saw in Napoleon the incarnation of what he later dubbed 'the World Spirit'. In a letter to a friend, he writes that with the completed manuscript of *The Phenomenology of Spirit* lying on his desk,

> *'... on the night of October 13, 1806, I saw outside of my study the camp-fires of Napoleon's occupation forces... Next day, I saw* die Weltseele *('The World Spirit') on horseback marching through the city of Jena.'*

It's a nice image, almost journalistic, and, in fact, Hegel had a brief period as a newspaper editor. Otherwise, Hegel devoted his life wholly to teaching, first at Jena, then Nuremberg, Heidelberg, and finally Berlin.

The first two posts were in schools. Only the latter ones (from 1816) were as the university 'professor' that he is congenitally depicted as, and in fact his key writings date from his earlier school-masterly time.

If Hegel looks rather unappealing

The Emperor Napoleon, whom Hegel saw riding through Jena.

in the portraits we have of him, an even more unappetising image is portrayed by one of his students who recalls his lectures thus:

'There he sat, with relaxed, half-sullen air, and, as he spoke, kept turning backwards and forwards the leaves of his long folio manuscript; a constant hacking and coughing disturbed the even flow of speech; every proposition stood isolated by itself, and seemed to force its way out all broken and twisted; every word, every syllable was, as it were, reluctantly let go, receiving from the metallic ring of the broad Swabian dialect a strange emphasis, as if it were the most important thing to be said.'

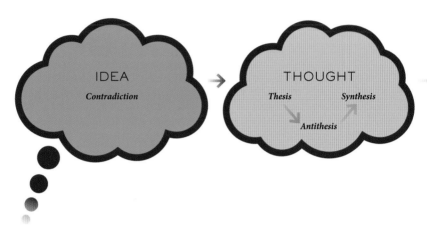

Hegel's first and most celebrated major work is the *Phenomenology of Spirit* (or sometimes just *Mind*).

During his life he also published many other works including the *Encyclopaedia of the Philosophical Sciences, the Science of Logic* and the well-named *Philosophy of Right*.

Like Kant, Hegel's writing is notorious for being hard work and, again like Kant, he is certainly ambitious in the range of the topics he attempts to cover.

The key to understanding reality is, for Hegel, the principle of contradiction – which, indeed, is a principle that Kant uses to some good effect in his brief discussion of certain paradoxes, or 'antimonies'.

Kant offers the antimonies almost as a tasty aperitif, but for Hegel, (following the spirit of the Ancients) contradiction is the way to philosophical insights.

When an idea is found to contain within it a contradiction, the search is

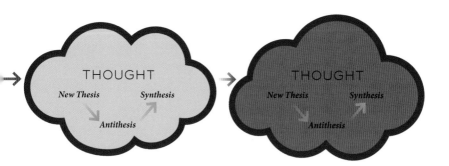

triggered for a way to resolve it, and in the process, thought itself is forced to develop and move to a higher stage.

Hegel calls the process dialectical reasoning. It consists of a thesis, which inevitably generates an antithesis, and the two ideas then must fight it out until a new, better theory combines the old ideas in a synthesis.

The process is ongoing as the synthesis, once it is established, soon becomes itself a new thesis, generating its own antithesis, and then the search for a new synthesis must take place.

This kind of paradoxical reasoning inspired Hegel, who adopted the style for all his own writing, presenting issues in what he called dialectical form.

By this he meant producing one view, presenting an opposed view and then, like a conjuror producing the rabbit, coming up with a third view that manages to reconcile the conflict.

Hegel did not view the French Revolution as a struggle for liberty.

SOCIETY BORN OF CONFLICT

Hegel applied his dialectical reasoning to all manner of issues – but undoubtedly the most influential claim he made was that human society proceeds in just this kind of evolutionary way.

For example, for Hegel, the origin of society is in the first conflict between two humans, a 'bloody battle' with each seeking to make the other recognise them as master, and accept the role of slave. Society is perpetually thereafter divided into the two classes: of slaves and masters (Did he mean a battle between a man and a woman? Unlikely, and he does not seem to have considered the issue).

However, it is not material need that propels one class to oppress the other – it is a conflict born solely out of the peculiarly human lust for power over one another. And the French Revolution was simply the slaves revolting.

Hegel, unlike, say, Thomas Hobbes, approves of the motivation, which he calls the 'desire for recognition'. For many, this risks death, but it is the only way towards 'freedom'. It's a funny sort of freedom, though. In the *Philosophy of Right*, Hegel writes:

> '*The history of the world is the discipline of the uncontrolled natural will, bringing it into obedience to a universal principle and conferring subjective freedom...* '

Hegel explains in excellent head-masterly style that the state doesn't exist for the individual, but rather the individual exists for the state.

Hegel's new society aims to combine both of the two totalitarian doctrines: fascism and communism. It is an illusion to think of anything as separate from anything else, and, in as much as we do so, our thinking is flawed. Actually, even 'the whole', which replaces all these imagined separate objects, is not essentially one substance, but many, just as an organism, such as the human body, is made up of different parts with their own characteristics and functions.

Hegel imagined a society functioning like a human body.

For Hegel, the correct approach to knowledge is not to think of truth and falsity but rather ideas which are only partially true, and those that edge nearer to truth. This he calls the 'Absolute' and linked to the politics of his time.

Even that most basic distinction between space and time – the Absolute – is also rather like God, (a rather austere kind of God). A quote, from Hegel's lectures on the Philosophy of History, gives the flavour:

> *'On the stage on which we are observing it – Universal History – Spirit displays itself in its most concrete reality.'*

It makes good sense, historically, that the most important consequences of Hegel's ideas were political. In particular, the adaptation of his dialectical reasoning and its application to human history by two radical thinkers: Karl Marx and Friedrich Engels.

Marx and Engels revisited Hegel's theory to produce their own, more

Karl Marx adapted Hegel's dialectical reasoning to develop and support his own ideas of how society should be structured.

positive (they thought) version, in which human class conflict comes to an end. Differences dissolve in a society of equal citizens, coordinated by a kindly and omniscient ruling Communist Party cadre.

Creating this ideal has been harder to realise than Marx and Engels anticipated, writing in the context of impoverished workers toiling in factories for a clearly identifiable ruling class.

'The history of all hitherto existing society is the history of class struggles.'
The Communist Manifesto

Let's look a bit closer at Engels, the figure less often discussed. Although less attention is lavished upon him, it is generally accepted that it was Engels, rather than Marx, who was the originator of the theory of dialectical materialism, the key point of which is to suppose that the conflict between the impoverished workers and the inherent failings of capitalism must lead to a new, radically egalitarian socialist world.

Friedrich Engels was a German social scientist and philosopher who developed The Communist Manifesto *along with Marx.*

STATE OF UTOPIA

It seems likely that Engels, nicknamed 'the General' in the Marx household, wrote the first draft of The Communist Manifesto.

He probably also wrote most of *The German Ideology*, a key reference text for the future revolutionaries, as well as many of the articles of agitprop that appeared under Marx's name in the newspapers. It was Engels who created the concept of 'Marxism' in another book called *Socialism: Utopian and Scientific*.

It was even Engels who did the vital work of assembling the various volumes of *Capital*, although this is believed to have been out of Marx's copious notes taken in many research trips to the British Library.

Unlike Hegel, Engels is firmly materialist. Material causes underlie natural phenomena, and so the evolution and development of society is driven by material factors. These he calls 'the forces of material production'. The relationships people enter into in the process of producing material goods explain all social phenomena.

The Communist Manifesto, *first edition, in German.*

'The first act by virtue of which the State really constitutes itself the representative of the whole of society – the taking possession of the means of production in the name of society – this is, at the same time, its last independent act as a State. State interference in social relations becomes, in one domain after another, superfluous, and then dies out of itself; the

Karl Marx did much of his research and writing in the British Museum Reading Room in London.

government of persons is replaced by the administration of things, and by the conduct of processes of production. The State is not "abolished."
It dies out.'

> *Socialism, Utopian and Scientific* (1880)

Similarly, in *The Poverty Of Philosophy* (1847) Marx puts it like this:

'In acquiring new productive forces men change their mode of production; and in changing their mode of production, in changing the way of earning their living, they change all their social relations. The hand-mill gives you society with the feudal lord; the steam-mill society with the industrial capitalist.'

Bill Clinton takes the oath of office from Chief Justice William Rehnquist during his 1993 presidential inauguration.

Socialism, for Marx and Engels, is not about what people want or about right and wrong, it is a practical matter. Socialism is simply the most efficient way to arrange the forces of production to promote human wellbeing.

Where Hegel sees ideas fighting it out for progress, Marx and Engels insist that ideas reflect economic, material forces and relations. Ideas do not drive revolutions, practical economics does.

In short, 'It's the economy, stupid,' as James Carville, the campaign strategist for Bill Clinton's successful 1992 presidential bid against sitting president George H. W. Bush almost put it.

Carville's idea was to turn voters away from the war in Iraq of which, at one point, 90 per cent of Americans approved.

A decade on, the war was a toxic legacy, of course, but then, as the saying goes, a week is along time in politics!

Although Marx and Engels always spring to mind when the question of who first undertook a philosophical examination of the capitalist system is posed, in fact, the key elements of the mechanisms of capitalism were earlier – and better – described by a much gentler thinker, Adam Smith (1723–1790).

In his incredibly popular book *The Wealth of Nations*, capitalism promotes the general good, and thus is not only the best possible system, but also produces the best possible world, a view comfortably reflected today by Western politicians.

Today, the sun has definitively set on much of Marxist theory, whereas Smith's terms and ideas continue to frame the economic debate and to be vigorously promoted – or opposed – by government economists.

The monument of Adam Smith outside St. Giles Cathedral, Edinburgh, Scotland.

THE WEALTH OF NATIONS

When the first edition of Adam Smith's An Inquiry into the Nature and Causes of the Wealth of Nations, *came out, coincidentally in the same year as the American Declaration of Independence, 1776, it cost the very princely sum of one pound and sixteen shillings, but still sold out within six months.*

Adam Smith explored the notion of self interest.

Smith's publisher, William Stahern, had just produced another best-seller, Gibbon's *Decline and Fall of the Roman Empire* and had at one point feared that the *Wealth of Nations* might be too technical for the popular readership of *Decline and Fall*. But Gibbon himself realised that there was a great strength in Smith's analysis and writing. 'It was there,' he wrote, 'in the most profound ideas expressed in the most perspicuous language.'

And it was there because the *Wealth of Nations* is, despite the title, not merely concerned with economics. It is a much more comprehensive vision of society, and in its pages economics is merely a by-product, albeit a necessary one, of social life.

So Smith is concerned not only with money, but with justice and equity. If his findings are nowadays adopted by those of a different disposition, that is not his fault.

Adam Smith is a much more radical philosopher than he is usually given credit for. Where earlier philosophers, such as Plato and John Locke, saw society as needing to be based on altruism, or at least (as in Hobbes) the suppression of selfishness, Smith is firmly in favour of it! Famously, it is not out of the benevolence of the butcher or the baker that we can expect our supper, it is from their enlightened notion of their own self interest.

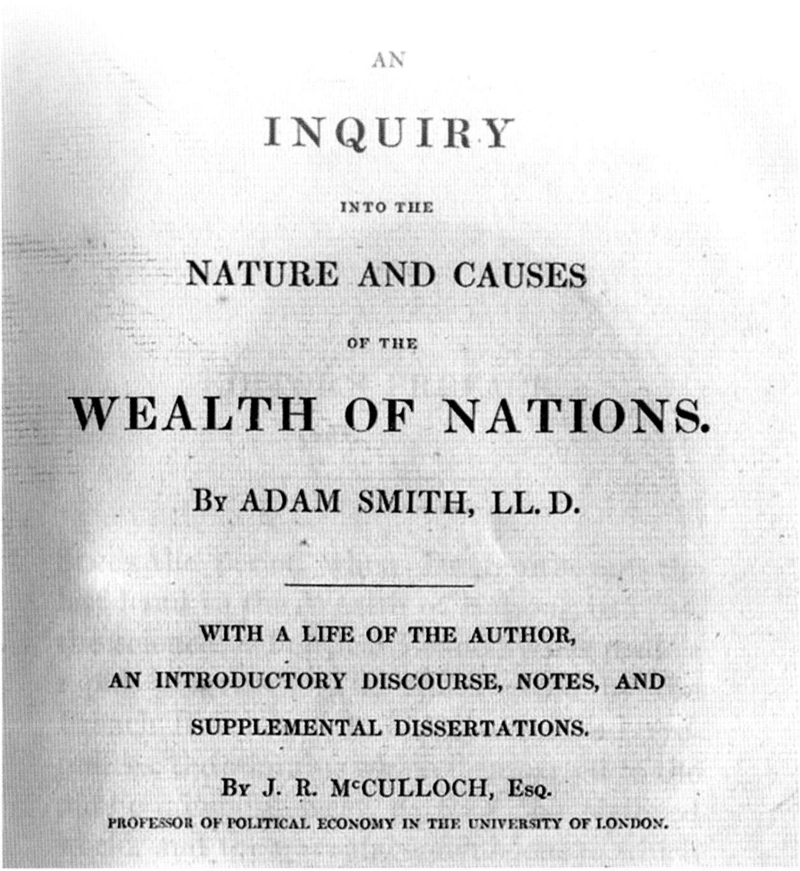

AN

INQUIRY

INTO THE

NATURE AND CAUSES

OF THE

WEALTH OF NATIONS.

By ADAM SMITH, LL. D.

———

WITH A LIFE OF THE AUTHOR,
AN INTRODUCTORY DISCOURSE, NOTES, AND
SUPPLEMENTAL DISSERTATIONS.

By J. R. M^cCULLOCH, Esq.
PROFESSOR OF POLITICAL ECONOMY IN THE UNIVERSITY OF LONDON.

The law of unintended social outcomes develops through Smith's phrase 'the invisible hand' by which:

'... every individual necessarily labours to render the annual revenue of the society as great as he can. He generally, indeed, neither intends to promote the public intent, nor knows how much he is promoting it...

Karl Marx, with whom Adam Smith had fundamental differences over human nature.

he intends only his own gain, and he is in this, as in many other cases, led by an invisible hand to promote an end which was no part of his intention.'

But where Marx and Engels saw human motivation as essentially practical, directed by physical needs for heat and food, Smith sees underlying it something essentially psychological, indeed moral.

'... it is chiefly from this regard to the sentiments of mankind that we pursue riches and avoid poverty. For to what purpose is all the toil and bustle of the world? What is the end of avarice and ambition, of the pursuit of wealth, of power, or pre-eminence?
'To be observed, to be attended to, to be taken notice of with sympathy, complacency, and approbation, are all the advantages which we can

propose to derive from it.
'It is the vanity, not the ease or the pleasure, which interests us.'

The Moral Sentiments

Along with the effects of varying corn prices (studies which also influenced Marx), Smith investigates human values, seeing moral behaviour as built up in the mind from the influence of parents, teachers, school fellows and society. The conscience acts as a kind of 'impartial spectator', watching and judging us.

Adam Smith saw co-operation guiding all aspects of the economy, even without people intending it.

Where Freud would allow the 'unconscious' still to lead us astray, Smith makes his impartial spectator, similar to that of Freud's Super Ego, determined to lead us towards the light.

There are four factors determining a person's respect for others: personal qualities, age, fortune and birth. The first is open to debate, so age is a better yardstick. Fortune, or wealth, is, Smith notes, a surprising source of respect. Rich people are admired and benefit in terms of social esteem just by their wealth, and equally, poor people lose out both ways.

Smith is aware of the possibility of self-deception, and curses it as the source of 'half of the disorders of human life'. If only, he wrote in *The Moral Sentiments*, we could see ourselves as others see us as then 'a reformation would be unavoidable. We could not otherwise endure the sight.'

Marx and Smith observed great wealth and desperate poverty in Victorian Britain.

'To judge your own behaviour requires you to – at least for a moment – to divide into two people, and one be the spectator of the actions of the other. Nature had endowed each of us with a desire not only to be approved of, but with a desire of being what ought to be approved of.'

The Moral Sentiments

But then people, Marx explains in the *Poverty of Philosophy*, are both the authors and the actors of their own drama – even,

Not even twins can see themselves as others see them, in the way that Adam Smith said we should all try to.

or perhaps particularly, philosophers. These 'do not spring up like mushrooms out of the ground,' Marx explains, this time in an editorial for the *Kölnische Zeitung*, but are likewise 'products of their time, of their nation, whose most subtle, valuable and invisible juices flow into the ideas of philosophy.'

A GREAT DOUBLE ACT

Given their impact on philosophy and on world politics, Karl Heinrich Marx and Friedrich Engels must go down as one of the greatest double acts of all time.

Karl Marx and Friedrich Engels came from distinctly different social backgrounds.

Karl Heinrich Marx was born in Trier (then in German Rhineland) and died in London 1883. In between he studied law at Bonn and Berlin but became enthralled by philosophy and history, applying Hegel's 'dialectical' method where everything generates its opposite, followed by a conflict in which a 'synthesis' must emerge.

Marx seems to have lived a rather sad and lonely life of, if not true poverty, straitened circumstances, apparently deeply affected by the early deaths of four of his seven children, from malnutrition and poor living conditions.

The son of a wealthy German lawyer, who had renounced his Jewish faith in order to progress in his career, he married the 'most beautiful girl in Trier', the daughter of the Baron of Westphalen, Jenny, to whom in due course it fell to pawn the family silver (marked with the crest of the Dukes of Argyll). She also had to cope with Marx's unfaithfulness, which produced an illegitimate child by one of their servants.

Jenny wrote and edited many of the revolutionary scripts, but how great an input Jenny Marx actually had, no one really knows.

Engels was the support system behind Marx, son of a textile manufacturer and owner of a factory in Manchester during the critical years following the failure of revolutions in much of Europe, including in Paris, Rome, Berlin, Vienna, Prague and Budapest. He originally wanted to be a writer of novels, but was obliged by his father to follow the family business instead. Of such things are revolutions made!

The two met originally in Berlin, in 1842, but it was not until two years later, and in Paris, that they began their lifelong collaboration. It was Engels who introduced Marx to the working class issues and the new philosophy of political science. Nonetheless, Engels himself always credited Marx with that important but nebulous quality, 'originality.'

Friedrich Engels' house in Primrose Hill, London.

Queen Victoria, her government and advisors were deeply concerned about the threat to the establishment from radical new political ideologies such as Marx and Engel's communism.

Marx and Engels reorganised the Communist League for its meeting in London in 1847 and co-wrote *The Communist Manifesto* in 1848, the year of revolutions in Europe.

It is this relatively short and colourful *Manifesto* for the embryonic Communist Party, written in German, printed in London and speedily translated into French in time for the insurrection in Paris of June 1848, that made their mark on history.

The Communist Manifesto opens with the famous promise: 'Let the ruling classes tremble at a communistic revolution. The proletarians have nothing to lose but their chains. They have a world to win!'

It goes on to portray society as a whole as increasingly 'splitting up into two great hostile camps, into two great classes directly facing each other: bourgeoisie and proletariat.' In one of the Manifesto's memorable phrases, Marx and Engels argue that 'the whole history of mankind is a series of bitter struggles between two classes:

Engels saw the class struggle in similar terms to the evolution of Man: for him it was the evolution of societies.

the exploited and the exploiting.'

This idea, as Engels ambitiously puts it in the preface to the 1888 English version of the Manifesto, is comparable to Darwin's theory of evolution. Marxism is the theory of the evolution of societies. It is as impersonal and its conclusions as inevitable as Darwin's biological model of the development of species.

Even today, 150 years on, if the proletariat, or full-time workers, are often the bourgeoisie too, the words still strike a chord. Equally, even as the workers are 'embourgoiseified', there has developed alongside what contemporary Marxists call the new 'unworking class' – casual labourers, the unemployed, the old, the mad and the sick – a new underclass. However, this class is not so much exploited as ignored and forgotten.

Another chord is struck when Marx and Engels continue by saying that when we examine the characteristics of the new industrial society, we see that the bourgeoisie has established itself as the supreme power in the modern state, running the government, turning it into 'but a committee for managing the affairs of the whole bourgeoisie'.

Marxism is a conflict theory, and Marx himself was no diplomat. He saw and created enemies everywhere. He fell out with the French authorities and, on being expelled from Paris, instead declared himself to be 'a citizen the world'.

After settling briefly in Brussels, he then fell out with the Belgians, who accused him (probably correctly) of supplying money to the Belgian workers for weapons to start an uprising.

He fell out with the anarchists, in general and the Russian revolutionary, Mikhail Bakunin, in particular over the question of whether the communist vanguard would usher in the classless society, or simply degenerate into

The tombstone of Karl Marx in Highgate Cemetery, London, England.

a corrupt, cruel and incompetent bureaucracy.

And then *The Communist Manifesto*, with its call for revolutions, of course made Marx unwelcome in Germany. So, in 1849, Marx and Jenny (and their children and their 'loyal housekeeper') retreated to

London instead where they would wait the rest of their lives in disappointment for the workers to rise up in the countries that had rejected them.

This was the London of Charles Dickens' novels, of dark satanic mills; of grim workhouses where Oliver Twists were refused more porridge; a London where barefoot children struggled to fend for themselves.

Vintage engraving showing poverty in 19th-century London.

Predominantly female workers in a Victorian jam factory – it would appear to be dangerous, hot and sticky work.

It is clear that, rather than dwell on human stories, Marx and Engels were more concerned about their quasi-religious theory of how society changes.

Engels was, after all, a factory owner himself, but their belief in their own theory explains why Marx's writings are a substitute for physical activity – revolutionary or otherwise. In a way, he was a great snob, embittered by personal experience. Just before his death he observed that he was 'the best-hated and most calumniated man of his time.'

The hammer and sickle, the symbol of Communism, on the USSR flag.

COMMUNISM'S REVOLUTIONARY INGREDIENTS

The 'generally applicable' requirements of communist revolution, as offered by the Manifesto in pocket summary form are:

- Abolition of land ownership and rents
- A heavy progressive income tax
- Abolition of all inheritance rights
- Confiscation of the property of all those who no longer live in the state, or who rebel against the new government
- Centralisation of all capital and credit in a state bank
- Central state control and ownership of the means of communication and transportation
- Increased state production through factories and farming: development of under-used land
- 'Equal liability of all to labour' – new armies of workers
- Disappearance of the distinction between town and country: population distributed evenly over the country

And, lastly:

- Free education for all in state-run schools, preparing the children for work in the new industries.

CHAPTER 8

A FORK IN THE ROAD: PHILOSOPHIES OF ROMANTICISM AND HUMAN STRIVING

'The ultimate aim of all love affairs… is more important than all other aims in man's life; and therefore it is quite worthy of the profound seriousness with which everyone pursues it.'

Schopenhauer, *The World as Will and Representation*
(Supplements to the Fourth Book)

The German philosopher, Arthur Schopenhauer.

SYSTEM BREAKERS

If you look in standard textbooks, philosophy is one long discovery of rationality and logic, with the happy ending being professional philosophers in universities.

Well, that's the version written by the professors! But there is another side to the story, which stars quite different names and points in a very different direction. It is a defiantly non-academic, but much more literary, style of philosophy, and among its fruits are many key insights into human nature and motivations.

Statue of the Danish philosopher, Søren Kierkegaard.

In the previous chapter, we considered three of the great system builders of philosophy: Kant, Hegel and Marx, all determined to 'once and for all' determine the rules that govern not only human society – in itself an ambitious project – but the universe as well.

This chapter will look at three of the less-celebrated but equally influential system-breakers: the Danish iconoclast Søren Kierkegaard; the black sheep of German language philosophy, Arthur Schopenhauer, and the flamboyant Swiss-French philosopher, Jean-Jacques Rousseau

First let's take the great romantic, Jean-Jacques Rousseau – quite possibly the most eloquent writer of them all. Rousseau fought against conventional philosophy on every front, just as Leibniz in his way did. For Rousseau, Descartes'

Jean-Jacques Rousseau in a romantic pose in 1753.

Cogito is a source of corruption, not a fount of truth. 'I is not Me', he insists. I feel, therefore I am. I think, only leads me to think that you are.

If, for Thomas Hobbes, 'me-ism' made man greedy and fearful – Rousseau makes of it 'a divine spark' placed in every human breast, that elevates freedom above all other considerations. This is a freedom composed of three parts: free will, freedom from the rule of law (as ideally there are no laws), and personal freedom.

279

Rousseau points out that much of the imagery in the English philosophies of both Hobbes and Locke belongs only to a property-owning society – and Rousseau (as the Marxists would later also do) sees property as the usual cause and root of most problems.

Instead, Rousseau praises a vanished, pre-industrial world in which people grazed like animals on the fruits of nature and conflict was banished. His fellow countryman, the highly respected writer, Voltaire, mocked Rousseau, saying that his philosophy would require him to 'walk on all fours'.

Yet Rousseau's message resonated and contributed to the groundswell of the French and American revolutions.

> 'Society is produced by our wants, and government by wickedness; the former promotes our happiness positively by uniting our affections, the latter negatively by restraining our vices. The one encourages intercourse, the other creates distinctions. The first is a patron, the last a punisher.'
>
> Thomas Paine,
> *Common Sense* (1776)

Rousseau is one of the great philosophical optimists. Arthur Schopenhauer is one of philosophy's great pessimists. In a book, appropriately enough called *On the Suffering of the World*, he even advises that:

> 'The best consolation in misfortune or affliction of any kind will be the thought of other people who are in a still worse plight than yourself; and this is a form of consolation open to every one. But what an awful fate this means for mankind as a whole! We are like lambs in a field, disporting themselves under the eye of the butcher, who chooses out first one and then another for his prey.'

Thomas Paine, the 'Philosopher of the American Revolution', whose ideas were greatly influenced by those of Jean-Jacques Rousseau.

HUMAN PUPPETS

Schopenhauer's depressing but plausible insight is that human freedom is largely imagined – and that the reality is that we are all mere puppets.

As puppets, our actions are determined in a large part by hidden genetic promptings, developed over countless millennia of biological evolution. It is Schopenhauer, not more recent commentators like Richard Dawkins, who really discovered the 'selfish gene'.

And what of the Danish philosopher, Søren Kierkegaard? He is also somewhat pessimistic in outlook. Writing in one of his witty and complex books, called rather confusingly *Either/Or*, he warns that:

'Most men rush after pleasure so fast that they rush right past it. They are like that dwarf that guarded a kidnapped princess in a castle. One day he took a noon nap. When he woke up an hour later, she was gone. Hastily, he pulls on his seven-league boots; with one step he is far past her.'

Kierkegaard's point is made clearer when he talks about seeking happiness by drinking wine! It no longer cheers his heart, a little of it instead makes him sad.

'My soul is dull and slack, in vain do I jab the spur of desire into its side... If I were to wish for something, I would wish not for wealth or power but for the passion of possibility... pleasure disappoints, possibility does not.'

There is a depth and subtlety to all three philosophers that has made their writing grow in influence over the centuries, so let's start by looking a little closer at Rousseau – one of the most misunderstood thinkers of them all.

Kierkegaard used the drinking of wine to make philosophical points about happiness and misery.

It was only at age 38, rather late by the standards of many philosophers, that Jean-Jacques Rousseau underwent a profound period of sudden insights. The catalyst for this was seeing an advertisement offered by the Academy of Dijon for a prize

Rousseau sold his watch, saying he had no need to tell the time.

essay on the subject 'Have the arts and sciences benefited mankind?'

A flurry of ideas came to him and Rousseau wrote them down furiously. Science, literature and art were all 'bad' he decided, acid that eats into morals. They contribute to a culture of acquisition, of unsatisfied desires, which can only lead, in due course, to conflict, slavery and subjugation. And every strand of knowledge is derived from a sin: geometry comes from avarice; physics from vanity and empty curiosity; astronomy from superstition. Ethics itself is rooted in pride. Scientists, he says, far from being our saviours, are ruining the world, and any notion of progress they bring with their discoveries and inventions is an illusion that spreads even as we move further and further away from the healthy, simple and balanced lives of the past.

The essay was like a breath of fresh air in the stale debates of the time and, what is rather more surprising, Rousseau won the prize. Propelled thus from obscurity to celebrity, he began to adopt new patterns of behaviour more fitting to his essayist views. He developed a love for long walks and quiet contemplation of the countryside and he eschewed all sophistication and technology.

He even sold his watch saying he no longer needed to know the time.

Statue of Jean-Jacques Rousseau in Geneva, Switzerland, where he was born.

INSTITUTIONS OF EVIL

Rousseau also wrote an equally good follow-up essay, entitled A Discourse on Inequality *but this, alas, failed to win a prize, despite being every bit as controversial.*

Rousseau's anti-establishment views were not popular with the Catholic Church.

In it, he explains that 'man is naturally good, and only by institutions is he made bad', a view that could be expected to displease the all-powerful Church, in all its Catholic and Protestant hues (and making it almost certain that he would not win).

In the Discourse, like Thomas Hobbes, he uses an imaginary 'State of Nature' to infer certain 'natural laws', only upon which can the state establish its own order. Like Hobbes, too, he says that men are essentially equal, even accepting evident differences due to health, intelligence, strength and so on. So what explains the differences between individuals seen in society? The answer is:

'... the extreme inequality of our ways of life, the excess of idleness among some and the excess of toil among others, the ease of stimulant and gratifying our appetites and senses, the over elaborate foods of the rich, which inflame and overwhelm them with indigestion, the bad food of the poor which they often go without altogether, so that they over-eat greedily when they have the opportunity; those late nights, excesses of all kinds, immoderate transports of every passion, fatigue, exhaustion of the mind, the innumerable sorrow as and anxiety that people in all classes suffer, and by which the human soul is constantly tormented...'

The origins of inequality are, thus, unnatural, stemming from the institution of private property. In short, Rousseau says that the 'first man who, having enclosed a piece of land, thought of saying "this is mine," and found people simple enough to believe him, was the real founder of civil society.'

According to Rousseau, all the problems of society, including poverty, could be blamed on the institution of private property.

Rousseau's views on society were borrowed by Marx, who used a quote from Rousseau's book the *Social Contract* to front *The Communist Manifesto*:

> *'Man is born free, and everywhere he is in chains.'*

Better, Rousseau says, that people be measured not by their social position, nor by their possessions, but by the shared divine spark that he sees in them all: the immortal soul of 'Natural Man'. This is truly a Copernican revolution in political thought!

In both the *Social Contract*, and in the *Discourse on Inequality*, Rousseau argues that man in his natural state is living in a peaceful, contented state, truly free. Rousseau paints a mocking portrait of the social contract offered by the rich man, seeking to protect his gains by pretending concern for his victims.

Let us unite, says his rich man, to protect the weak from oppression, to ensure for each that which he owns, and create a system of justice and peace that all shall be bound to, without exception. Yet the poor have only one thing – their freedom – and to voluntarily strip themselves of that without gaining anything in exchange would appear to be absolute folly. The rich, on the other hand, have much to gain.

Rousseau thinks his explanation of civil law is much more convincing than those offered by philosophers who suppose some other sort of universal social contract,

Writing a century later, Nietzsche choked over all this. In his notebook for

Discourse on the Origin and Foundations of Inequality Among Men by Jean-Jacques Rousseau.

Rousseau frequented the Café Florian in Venice, as did Goethe, Casanova, Byron, Proust and Dickens, although not all at the same time.

Autumn 1887, otherwise preoccupied with lamenting the abolition of slavery and the propaganda of treating people as 'equal', Nietzsche speaks of his struggle against Rousseau and his notion of natural man as good. It is a philosophy born, Nietzsche declares fiercely, 'out of a hatred of aristocratic culture'.

For Rousseau, there is only one way around this conflict, only one way that the sovereign and the people can have a single and identical interest and ensure that all the 'movements of the civil machine' tend to promote the common happiness, and that is for them to be one and the same. The people must be sovereign.

Rousseau died in 1778, the same year as his rival and critic, Voltaire, possibly by his own hand, and certainly in sad and lonely circumstances. Yet as Goethe perceptively commented: with Voltaire an age ended, but with Rousseau, a new one began.

The general will, in Rousseau's use of the term, is the collective wishes of everyone, directed to common

Detail of the monument to Jean-Jacques Rousseau in the Pantheon, Paris.

interests, and is quite distinct from the 'consensus view' which is merely the aggregate of many individual selfish wishes and desires. He describes the essence of it:

> *'Each of us puts his person and all his power in common under the supreme direction of the general will, and, in our corporate capacity, we receive each member as an indivisible part of the whole.'*

Rousseau's social contract thus still includes an element of obligation – one chain remains. The populace has a duty to obey 'the general will', as represented by the Sovereign. However, the Sovereign, in Rousseau's society, is not an individual or a party, but all the people, collectively taken.

Rousseau proposes that we exchange a negative, personal liberty that allows us to follow our desires wherever they take us, for a superior kind of positive liberty, which is obtained by electing to follow the general will.

Rousseau urged individuals to choose to follow the will of the population rather than their own desires.

THE DARK SIDE

Rousseau builds his philosophy on an optimistic view of human nature.
Schopenhauer, on the other hand, builds his on the opposite assumption.

Monument to the German philosopher Arthur Schopenhauer in Bremen's Wallanlagen Park.

Schopenhauer is a much underrated thinker, often left out of standard lists of 'the great philosophers', and sometimes not even included as one of the great German philosophers. This is despite his undoubted influence on the psychological theories of Sigmund Freud, Friedrich Nietzsche and on to Ludwig Wittgenstein.

He regularly and violently assailed academic philosophy, saying:

'Governments make of philosophy a means of serving their state interests, and scholars make of it a trade.'

Professional philosophy was, for him, epitomised by the detested Hegel, whom he called (among other unkind things):

'...a flat-headed, insipid, nauseating, illiterate charlatan, who reached the pinnacle of audacity in scribbling together and dishing up the craziest, mystifying nonsense'.

Schopenhauer adds that Hegel was paid by the monarch of Prussia to play 'jiggery-pokery' in front of an 'audience of fools', firmly putting himself on 'the other side' not only of most of his contemporaries, but of philosophers ever since.

The only academic philosopher that Schopenhauer had any time for was Kant, but even then, he considered his predecessor to have been basically mistaken.

Schopenhauer takes up Kant's argument that there is a more fundamental reality hidden behind the superficial world of appearances, which is, after all, a core idea in Eastern philosophy.

Kant insists that we can have no knowledge of this deeper reality – the noumenal world – but Schopenhauer offers that there is a way.

'It is, so to speak, a subterranean passage, a secret alliance, which, as if by treachery, places us all at once in the fortress that could not be taken by attack from without.'

The World as Will and Representation

Schopenhauer believed there was a 'secret passage' to the hidden reality of the world.

Schopenhauer was known as a womaniser and once tried to woo a young lady by offering her a bunch of grapes.

The secret passage is discovered by realising that our inner selves, our consciousness, is part of this other world. The subjective 'I' marks its presence through its interaction with the phenomenal word, the everyday world, while remaining itself a mystery.

Schopenhauer thinks, again in line with the Eastern mystics, that consciousness is, in fact, a universal force, not an individual characteristic. He allows that animals and even physical objects share it.

He argues that we can only

conceptualise things in the world around us, be it a tree or a bunch of tasty grapes or… an attractive young girl (he was a great womaniser) in so much as we locate them in a framework of time and space. But Kant's position is that time and space are human constructs, part of the phenomenal world and not part of underlying reality.

Yet, once time and space are removed, Schopenhauer points out, so too is the possibility of any particular things. The noumenal world, whatever it is and whatever it contains, has, literally, 'nothing in it'! Because it has no parts. It is not nothing, but is rather an undifferentiated something.

In the phenomenal word, of things, there can be cause and effect, but in the noumenal world, there cannot be. Such relations have no place there. The underlying reality does not 'cause' our experiences, as Kant seems to have assumed.

It is subjective awareness that provides the only access to the noumenal world. As Descartes intuited, there is a difference between the awareness of thoughts, and impressions via sense perception. But the awareness of thoughts has a particular character. It reveals itself as the life force, the will.

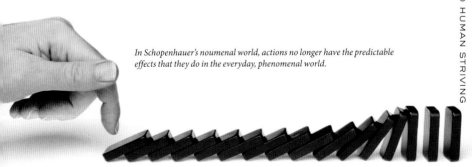

In Schopenhauer's noumenal world, actions no longer have the predictable effects that they do in the everyday, phenomenal world.

Schopenhauer does not place 'will', this universal striving, on a philosophical pedestal, though. It drives the universe, yes, and is the cause of all positive achievements and actions, but it is also the cause of all suffering.

Schopenhauer's compromise solution is to retreat whenever possible from the battles of the everyday world and seek to 'quell the strivings of the will' through quiet contemplation. He recommends this be done through art and music – the mystics, of course, recommend meditation.

It is in this context that a certain question may come to mind: Is it really true that Schopenhauer actually pushed an old lady down the stairs?

Schopenhauer recommended music as a way of quelling the 'strivings of the will'.

Ah, and this is indeed an interesting question concerning what is known, in legal circles anyway, as 'The Marquet Affair.' It certainly seems that Schopenhauer had rather a bad temper which drove him to do nasty (well, hasty) things occasionally – which is only illustrative of his philosophical theory, of course.

History records that, returning home one day, Schopenhauer found three of (what he considered) that nasty sub-species – women – gossiping outside his door. Schopenhauer apparently tried to push one of these, Caroline Louise Marquet (a seamstress who rented another room in the house) forcibly away, causing her to fall down the stairs.

It sounds pretty bad for Schopenhauer. But curiously, when Mrs Marquet, brought an action against him for damages, alleging that he had

Schopenhauer was found guilty of pushing an old lady down the stairs.

kicked and beaten her, Schopenhauer managed to convince the Court that whatever had happened (and he admitted using force) it was justified.

The Court dismissed the case. Only later, when she appealed against the judgment, and he declined to testify in his defence, was he found guilty and fined.

An illustration of a fairy tale by the Brothers Grimm who Schopenhauer met as a young man.

CHARLATAN PROFESSOR

The story of the court case against Schopenhauer illustrates, in an odd sort of way, his idea of people being puppets controlled by irrational impulses.

Schopenhauer's views are colourful and original, and his background is unusual too. He was born in what is today Poland, the son of a rich merchant, Heinrich Floris Schopenhauer, and Johanna Troisner, a glamorous and successful writer (of romantic novels) and socialite.

Heinrich was an anglophile who named his son Arthur in the hope that the English name would help him into a career in business. The Anglicisation strategy included taking out a subscription to the London *Times* and sending the young Schopenhauer to boarding school in London, but this plan collapsed as Arthur hated the school.

At 17, he was in Hamburg when his father threw himself into the river, apparently because of financial problems. Schopenhauer was devastated and seems to have blamed his mother with a resentment that only increased, as in the years following her husband's death she went from strength to strength, gaining a national reputation.

It was through her that Schopenhauer was introduced to many of Germany's great writers of the time, including Goethe, Schlegel, and the Brothers Grimm – as well as to the art of writing. It was at the University in Berlin that he first came into contact with mainstream philosophy – and he did not like it.

One of his professors was the celebrated Johann Fichte (1762–1814)

and he decided at once that the man was a charlatan. In his last book, *Parerga and Paralipomena* (1851) he explains:

> *'Fichte, Schelling and Hegel are in my opinion not philosophers, for the yack the first requirement of a philosopher, namely a seriousness and honesty of enquiry. They are merely sophists who wanted to appear to be, rather than to be, something. They sought not truth but their own interest and advancement.'*

Johann Fichte, Schopenhauer's tutor.

It seemed to Schopenhauer that the Eastern philosophers had greater insights into reality than any of his European contemporaries. His study contained, alongside a bust of Kant, and several portraits of doggy friends, a golden Buddha on a marble stand, while his library included more than 130 items of Oriental philosophy including sacred Hindu texts.

He is one of very few European philosophers to relate his work equally to Eastern as well as Western works.

Inspired by the writings of Easter thinkers, he saw himself as a metaphysical cryptographer who had stumbled upon the key to understanding the universe.

In *On the Vanity of Existence* he explains:

> 'The vanity of existence is revealed in the whole form existence assumes: in the infiniteness of time and space contrasted with the finiteness of the individual in both; in the fleeting present as the sole form to which actuality exists; in the contingency and relativity of all things in continual becoming without being; in continual desire without satisfaction; in the continual frustration of striving in which life consists.
>
> 'Time and that probability of all things existing in time that time itself brings about is simply the form under which the will-to-live, which as a

Schopenhauer had a golden statue of Buddha in his study.

Schopenhauer had a high regard for Eastern philosophy.

thing-in-itself is imperishable, reveals to itself the vanity of its striving. Time is that by virtue of which everything becomes nothingness in our hands and loses all real value.'

And in *The World as Will and Representation*, written in a non-academic style, with an ironic, aristocratic tone, Schopenhauer makes subjectivity the key to understanding the universe.

Desire, instinct, 'will' is the basic force. Life is meaningless, since birth leads to death and the only purpose of activity between the two seems to be to produce offspring who can then repeat the cycle.

There is nothing behind it – no strategy, no reason, no purpose. It is not only outside space and time, it creates these regularities, these 'appearances'. It is primary, it sweeps perception before

According to Schopenhaeur, the rabbit's inner fears determine its outward appearance.

it, it determines our concepts, it dictates all actions.

It even drives evolution, not the other way around as Darwin would have it. Animals reflect their innermost attitudes in their outwardly forms: thus the timid rabbit has its large ears, always ready to detect the faintest whiff of danger, while the cruel hawk, always hoping to tear other creatures apart, has a terrifying beak and talons.

Will is also irrational; it can create reasons but is by no means bound by them. The will to live and the will to procreate are irrational, they obey no rules and accept no logic. To demonstrate this, Schopenhauer uses the grisly example of the Australian ant, which, when decapitated, turns into two grotesque fighting machines. The head determined to bite the thorax, which in turn attempts to sting the other half to death.

It was only the second edition of *The World as Will and Representation* (in 1844) that received any public appreciation. Hitherto, Schopenhauer had been known, if at all, only as the son of the celebrated Johanna Schopenhauer; but now he came to have his own following which, if small at first, was certainly distinguished.

Schopenhauer used the example of a decapitated ant turning on itself to show that the will to live is irrational.

CELEBRITY STATUS

His celebrity was confirmed when a bust of him was made by Elizabeth Ney; the April 1853 number of the Westminster Review *grandly announced the arrival of a new writer and thinker in an article entitled 'Iconoclasm in German Philosophy.'*

The great Richard Wagner sent him a copy of his *Der Ring der Nibelungen*, with the inscription, 'In admiration and gratitude.'

With this success, Schopenhauer began to live as an aristocrat too, adopting a self-consciously leisurely existence as a 'great thinker'. Following the style of Kant, he dressed in an old-fashioned way, ate at strictly regular times, and took a daily walk with a much-loved poodle, which he called Atma, after the Hindu life-force or soul.

He sought to become the model of a scholarly recluse, content to study quietly in the library all day with just the occasional visit to the theatre or the public library for excitement. Asked once why he had originally abandoned the business career his parents had planned for him, he replied, 'Life is a difficult question; I have decided to spend my life in thinking about it.'

On the other hand, if we're talking about desire and the ego, and we are, it should be mentioned that Schopenhauer did manage to fit several relationships

The composer Richard Wagner was a fan of Schopenhauer's work.

Schopenhauer had a poor opinion of marriage, although he had several relationships.

into his life as a recluse, and even had an illegitimate son, whom, to this extent following the philosophical traditions, he ignored and allowed to die young from neglect. But then Schopenhauer didn't want to marry the mother anyway.

In his writings, he sneers that marriage is a debt, contracted in youth and paid off in old age. Had not all the true philosophers been celibates — Descartes, Leibniz, Malebranche, Spinoza, and Kant he opines?

For most of his life, no one was interested in Schopenhauer, let alone his philosophy of existence.

In fact, that first book was so widely ignored that despite only a few copies being printed, 16 years later most of them ended up as waste paper, as his publisher had warned they might.

The only consolation was the note his sister had written to him to say that Goethe 'had received it with great joy,

The German writer Johann Wolfgang Von Goethe was an admirer of Schopenhauer.

immediately cut the thick book, and began instantly to read it.'

Nonetheless, with the first edition selling only a few hundred copies, Schopenhauer was ill-tempered enough to write a bitter yet pompous preface to the second edition, dedicating his book not to his contemporaries, not to his compatriots, but to mankind 'in the confidence that it will not be without value for them, even if this should be late recognised, as is commonly the lot of what is good.'

And, in fact, years later, Friedrich Nietzsche would find a copy of *Die Welt als Wille und Vorstellung* in a second-hand bookstore, and be unable to put the book down until he had finished it.

Sigmund Freud would study Schopenhauer's description of the primal 'will to live' and 'sexual impulse' closely, before drawing up his own account of the 'life-instinct' and the centrality of the 'libido' in human life. Freud downplayed Schopenhauer's importance in his theories, but the similarities are very clear to anyone who cares to look.

Sigmund Freud was heavily influenced by Schopenhauer's work.

It is in no small part due to him that today the 'selfish gene' is regularly trotted out by pundits and scientists, that the 'will to power' features prominently in the writings of Nietzsche, and that the whole idea of individual desires and choices was polished up into a new kind of philosophy called existentialism.

Schopenhauer contrasts the way individuals die, 'but the sun itself burns without intermission'.

itself burns without intermission, an eternal noon. Life is certain to the will-to-live; the form of life is endless present; it matters not how individuals, the phenomenal of the Idea, arise and pass away in time, like fleeting dreams.'

The title of 'Father of Existentialism' instead is given to Søren Kierkegaard, the Danish philosopher born in Copenhagen, on 5 May, 1813. In the 'letter from the young aesthete', which is part of *Fear and Trembling*, one of his strange multilayered works, he revisits the important day saying:

Yet, even amongst existentialists, Schopenhauer's contribution is not appreciated. Fittingly perhaps, because, in *The World as Will and Representation*, he writes:

'The earth rolls on from day into night; the individual dies; but the sun

> 'I stick my finger into existence –
> it smells of nothing.
> Where am I?
> What is this thing called the world?
> Who is it that has lured me into the thing, and now leaves me here?
> Who am I?
> How did I come into the world?
> Why was I not consulted?'

These are good questions, and definitely existentialist ones. In his writings (like Rousseau, like Schopenhauer) Kierkegaard explicitly challenges mainstream philosophy since the Greeks, and its efforts to make sense of the world either through pure reason or through physical exploration and science. He says that neither of these approaches take into account the reality of human existence – life is about wants and desires, and choices.

Religion offers a set of answers to these life decisions, which makes it valuable. However, it must not be the kind of religion offered by Augustine and Aquinas, based on arguments and proofs. These reduce religion to an intellectual exercise. Nor can it be religion selected by adherence to rituals and institutional rules, because it is perfectly possible to be very good at adhering to these without having any personal religious insight or conviction.

Kierkegaard argued that religion often offered more answers than conventional philosophy.

GLOOMY UPBRINGING

When you look at his philosophical interests, it is no surprise to find that Søren Kierkegaard was born and brought up in a wealthy but dour Protestant household in which family life was punctuated by lessons in 'obedience' from the Bible.

His father, Michael Kierkegaard, liked to dwell morosely at the dinner table on the sufferings of Jesus and the martyrs, and the need for unquestioning obedience to God contained quintessentially in the story of Abraham.

This is the dreadful story in which Abraham is instructed by God to sacrifice not a sheep or a goat – but his

Depiction of Abraham about to sacrifice his son.

only son! Abraham, being a devout sort of chap, was ready to do it but, happily, at the very last minute, he received divine dispensation to 'stay his hand.'

The Kierkegaards were all members of the Moravian Church, a Christian sect that held, amongst other things, that the enjoyment of sex was sinful and that men should be allocated marriage partners by lottery.

Despite being so devout, Kierkegaard's father was burdened with dreadful guilt, officially due to his having once, as a young shepherd, cursed God.

Unofficially, though, he might have had pangs of remorse for apparently marrying a woman for money rather than for anything else, hurrying her into her grave just two years later, and then having an illegitimate baby with the maid, who later became Søren's mother. Whatever the reason, his religious devotion increased each year, as he tried to combat 'the curse' with faith.

A young Søren Kierkegaard shown studying at his desk.

He believed, in particular, that all of his family would perish before 34 years of age, that being the age at which Jesus died. Søren writes of both admiring and fearing his father with his grim preoccupation with death, and also of sometimes feeling that his 'insanity' was infecting the family.

Actually, for years, the dire prediction seemed to be becoming fulfilled. The first child died in a playground accident aged 12, and a sister, Maren, died at 25 of an unknown illness. She was soon followed by the other two daughters, Nicoline and Petrea, both in childbirth.

Niels tried to escape to America but died there aged 24. In fact, other than Søren himself, only one child managed to defeat the prophecy.

In his books, Kierkegaard offers long discussions of his father, but makes no mention of his mother or sisters. Otherwise, like his father, he is instead preoccupied directly with God.

Søren Kierkegaard's grave in Copenhagen, Denmark

Even as a young boy, Søren Kierkegaard was very serious. He lived in what is nowadays recalled as Denmark's 'Golden Age', but both Søren and his father were highly critical of the changes in society. They considered that serious values were being trivialised or lost.

Kierkegaard considered fireworks and other forms of public entertainment irreligious.

The superficiality of the 'new Denmark' was summed up for Søren by an amusement park established in Copenhagen. Here, peep shows, a wax museum, visual tricks such as dioramas, firework displays, and even pleasure gardens presented to him a frivolous, superficial and irreligious way of living. At Copenhagen's elite grammar school, the 'School of Civic Virtue', he was nicknamed 'The Fork', as he liked to pin down his classmates in intense debate and then expose inconsistencies in their arguments.

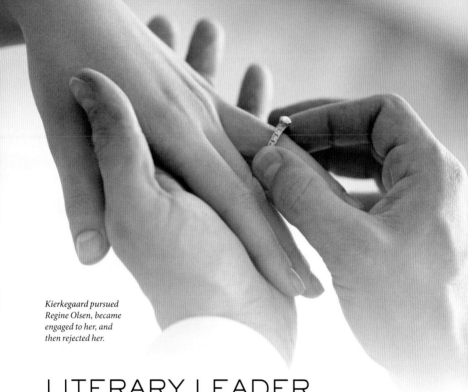

Kierkegaard pursued Regine Olsen, became engaged to her, and then rejected her.

LITERARY LEADER

Later, his interests shifted beyond merely winning arguments to becoming a leading figure in Copenhagen's literary world.

Søren directed all his energies into joining Copenhagen's most fashionable literary circle, starring one J.L. Heiberg, who had been responsible for introducing Hegel's philosophy to Denmark. Or almost all his energies.

It was at this time that Kierkegaard become engaged to Regine Olsen, whom he had first met when she was just 14.

INDIRECT COMMUNICATION

According to Kierkegaard, direct communication is a 'fraud' because it is related merely to objective thinking, and does not recognise the importance of subjectivity. Objectivity deprives readers of the use of their own views whereas indirect communication enables readers to bring in their own thoughts and to form a personal relation with ideas.

Christianity in particular, he writes, requires passion and an inner focus, which is essentially subjectivity. By comparison, supposedly objective philosophical constructions such as the truth offered by Hegel, the 'world-historical process', is cold and remorseless.

In his own writing, Kierkegaard stresses its subjectivity. He breaks up his texts into prefaces, preludes, preliminary explorations, interludes, postscripts, letters to the reader, collations by pseudonymous editors of pseudonymous sections, divisions and subdivisions in order to ensure that there is no obvious 'authoritative' point of view, but instead that the reader is obliged to use their own individual judgment about meaning.

And since Søren's books were 'self published' using his inheritance, he was able to write them any way he pleased and still have enough money left over for him to live in a comfortable and commodious six-room city suite with his faithful servant, Anders.

Søren Kierkegaard's house in Copenhagen, Denmark.

'Marriage is and remains the most important voyage of discovery a human being undertakes,' Kierkegaard explains, in *Stages on Life's Way.*

The romance with Regina became a theme of much of his writing, but not in a positive way. As he put it, in the words of Johannes the Seducer, one of his many pseudonyms, 'to poeticise oneself into a young girl is an art; to poeticise oneself out of her is a masterpiece.'

Kierkegaard's writing examined the nature of relationships in forensic detail.

Later, in the 'Diary of the Seducer' in *Either/Or*, he wrote:

> 'The awakening of sexual desire in adolescence makes our happiness lie outside ourselves, and its gratification dependent on the exercise of freedom by another. Sexual attraction fills us with heady delight, but also the dread of responsibility. Anxiety is this ambivalent oscillation between fascination and fear.'

So Regina had to go, but rather than gently and regretfully declare an end to the engagement, Søren set about humiliating her in public in the hope that she would then break off the relationship. Indeed, this is what eventually happened, and Regine went on to marry one of Søren's rivals, who later had a rather dull career as a diplomat.

Regina's humiliation had come in part through Kierkegaard's inclusion of racy accounts of their relationship in his philosophy, resulting in *Either/Or* becoming an instant success.

The Danish
author and poet,
Hans Christian
Andersen.

Even so, Søren never made it into the literary set. Frustration led him instead to less refined circles – including brothels and a group of heavy drinkers. This last group, however, included Hans Christian Andersen, already becoming a celebrated writer for his 'fairy tales'. Kierkegaard delighted in criticizing Andersen and his first proper publication was a critical examination of a Hans Christian Andersen novel, called *From the Papers of One Still Living.*

He did not, however, enjoy being criticized himself, which came after he challenged a satirical periodical called *The Corsair* to parody him. This it did very well, portraying him as an eccentric figure who wandered aimlessly around Copenhagen talking to people – and what's worse, whose trousers were too short!

Hurt by the mockery, Kierkegaard wrote in his journal: 'Geniuses are like thunder – they go against the wind, frighten people and clear the air'.

Today the waterside bars and restaurants of Copenhagen are bright and lively but in Kierkegaard's time they were far less refined.

CHOOSING YOUR DESTINY

It is in *Either/Or* that Kierkegaard sets out his new insight, that the essential choice we take is between sensuous self gratification or altruistic immersion in the demands of purity and virtue – the latter basically being the Christian commitment. And the choice cannot be made rationally, it is 'existential' in nature.

What does that mean? Well, existentialists say that such decisions define and create individuals: the person who takes them does not exist until after they have chosen. Thus they are beyond the rational judgement of others.

Søren applied this approach to Regina, creating what everyone else perceived as an elaborate series of public humiliations for the young woman, in order to 'provoke' her into ending their engagement. But, for Søren, he was creating the next Kierkegaard.

Whenever we decide to suspend the ethical, he writes egotistically, such acts will necessarily be beyond social justification and will be strictly 'ineffable'. They will be done in 'fear and trembling', (the title of another of his books) since they defy civic virtue and hover on the edge of madness.

THE JOURNALS
OF
SØREN
KIERKEGAARD

A SELECTION EDITED
AND TRANSLATED BY
ALEXANDER DRU

OXFORD UNIVERSITY PRESS
LONDON · NEW YORK · TORONTO
1938

Title page of 'The Journals of Soren Kierkegaard'.

CHAPTER 9
LANGUAGE, TRUTH AND LOGIC

'I really believe that languages are the best mirror of the human mind, and…
a precise analysis of the significations of words would tell us more than
anything else about the operations of our understanding.'

Leibniz, *New Essays*

A stained glass panel of St. Augustine in an Episcopal church, New York City, USA.

WORDS AND MEANINGS

For 2,000 years European thinkers had assumed that language merely followed thinking, and that thought was supposed to depend on laws of logic or reason.

They also assumed that those laws were supposed to be the same for everyone, no matter what language was used.

In the 4th century CE, St. Augustine summarised the view that had become a philosophical orthodoxy:

'*The individual words in language name objects – sentences are combinations of such names. In this picture of language we find the roots of the following idea: Every word has a meaning. This meaning is correlated with the word. It is the object for which the word stands.'*

Over the years it is the mathematically-minded philosophers, like Descartes, Leibniz, Russell and Frege, who have had a disproportionate influence. Disproportionate, that is, with regard to how many they are and with regard to the originality and value of their ideas. But influence they have had, even though Bertrand Russell and Gottlôb Frege, in fact, held that logic was superior to mathematics, which they attempted to reduce to a number of logical principles, without success.

The philosopher Bertrand Russell as a young man.

Take the case of Bertrand Russell, British philosopher, logician, essayist and social critic, who spent most of his professional life wrestling with the task of putting language on a 'logical foundation'.

Bertrand Russell's first important publication appeared in the philosophical journal *Mind* in 1905, and dealt with the workings of language. He called it *On Denoting*.

It is here that Russell outlines his vision of a new, more sensible, much simplified, logical language. Nouns such as 'girl', 'house', 'orchestra' or 'unicorn', when preceded by what Russell termed a 'quantifier', such as 'some', 'no', 'a', and 'every' become denoting phrases. Russell's proposal is that the quantifiers need to be done away with. This is because they do not really stand for anything.

A quantifier identifies a quantity, of course, but saying that also complicates things. Because to say a unicorn has one horn does not really mean that there really is a unicorn, which has one and only one horn.

Russell decided that everything we say must consist only of statements (perhaps combined) about things of which we have immediate direct knowledge – knowledge, quintessentially, by sense perception. Later on, he refined his approach by saying that all 'sensibilia' had to be understood as bundles of simple sense perceptions.

Russell narrowed these down as well, to things such as colours, smells, hardness, roughness and so on, a tactic which had occurred to many others before him to no great effect.

He says that 'sense-data' provides us with 'knowledge by acquaintance', otherwise we have to settle for 'knowledge by description'. Very little is given to us to know directly, even the existence of ourselves is limited to awareness of 'willing', 'believing', 'wishing' and so on. In a particularly curious example, Russell insists that mountains cannot be known directly, so we have to confine ourselves to talking about the sense perceptions we may have had which led us to create the 'hypothesis' of a mountain. Russell's house is surrounded by tall, hard objects which have snow on the top of them.

The only concession Russell allows, in line with best scientific practice, is that we may continue to make certain assumptions, such as that things continue to exist when not being looked at, and that what was true today continues to be true tomorrow, at least, 'in general'.

Just because it can be said that a unicorn has one horn, that doesn't mean it exists.

PHILOSOPHY HAVING PROBLEMS FINDING THE RIGHT WORDS

Another problem, for philosophers of language, concerns numbers. These are redesignated by Russell as mere adjectives. Two dogs, for example, is just another way of saying some dogs that have the quality of 'twoness'.

Same thing with my ears, your hands, Russell's first two wives and, in fact, every other group of things that has this binary quality. But what about Russell's other two wives (he had four)? Clearly another group of twoness. But the group of 'wives of Russell' has four members. Does it, too, belong in the group of two things? For it contains two collections of two wives. The philosophy of language is a complicated business.

Equally, as Russell put it in *Mind and Matter*, even simple sentences like 'snow is frozen water' need clarification, for what kind of verb is 'is'? (Two 'is' in a row there.) Is this 'is' an 'is' as in something exists? Or is 'is' is (that's three) as in 'equals'? Or is it 'is' as in describing a property of snow? Which is is it?

Two dogs or some dogs?

*The word 'beauty' can apply to many different
things, both natural and man-made.*

The classical approach to the philosophy of language starts by trying to impose a structure on the web of language. Nouns (and hence names) give an identity. This notion is central to Western philosophy.

The Ancient Greeks, as Plato's dialogues indicate, were fascinated by the way that a word, like 'chair' or 'beauty' can be applied to so many different things; things in which the property might only partially apply. Aristotle is concerned to set out the rules for using terms and, most importantly, how they can be joined together to express truths about the world.

LAWS OF THOUGHT

Aristotle's 'Laws of Thought', for example, which seemed to him then and still seem to many now, absolutely certain, start off by tidily asserting:

A equals A – law of identity

A does not equal 'not A' – law of non-contradiction

A equals either A or 'not A' but not both A and 'not A' – law of the excluded middle:

Actually, the laws go back well before Aristotle, who was essentially summarising the views of the pre-Socratic philosophers, most notably Parmenides.

The ancient Greek philosopher Heraclitus believed that seeing everything as being in a state of constant change was the key to understanding the universe.

It was he, in the 5th century BCE, who had formulated the second of the Laws as: 'Never will this prevail, that what is not, is'.

However, if saying something can't be both (say) white and not white at the same time, may seem uncontroversial, at the time, Parmenides' law actually represented a radical break with convention.

Up to then, the view of nature as a dynamic flux, in which things regularly changed into their opposites, had dominated. Heraclitus in particular had argued that since things changed, they had to contain what they were not. Only such contradictions could account for change.

The spiral shape in this petroglyph in Mesa Verde National Park, USA, probably represents the Sipapu, the place where the Hopi believe they emerged from the Earth.

Heraclitus' words have echoes of the language of the Ancient Chinese texts – and the Hopi Indians of North America (of which more in a moment). One Hopi saying is that: 'Cold things grow warm; warm grows cold; wet grows dry; parched grows moist.'

Ludwig Wittgenstein (who was Russell's doctoral student, although the two men cordially disliked each other), initially started off with Russell's view of language, which was the long-standing conventional view, but he later decided that language is, quite simply, a lot more complicated than that.

THE EASTERN PERSPECTIVE

Probably the first philosophical examination of the way that words and language shape reality comes not from the Western tradition but from the East.

In China, the School of Names (around 380 BCE) was concerned to explore the relationship of words to the world, while in India, Panini's *Sanskrit Grammar*, written around 350 BCE, uses a highly technical metalanguage consisting of a syntax, morphology and lexicon that is very much the approach of linguistics today.

The core of the text, called the *Ashtadhyayi*, consists of 3,959 sutras or rules, split into eight chapters, which are each subdivided into four sections called padas.

This key work was followed 400 years later by the *Patanjali*, or 'Great Commentary' assumed to be by several authors, which (again in technical style) discusses the nature of meaning.

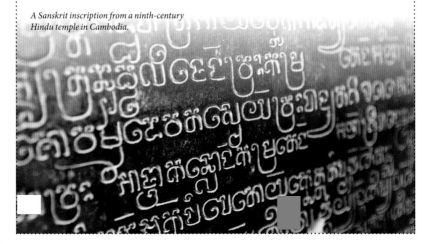

A Sanskrit inscription from a ninth-century Hindu temple in Cambodia.

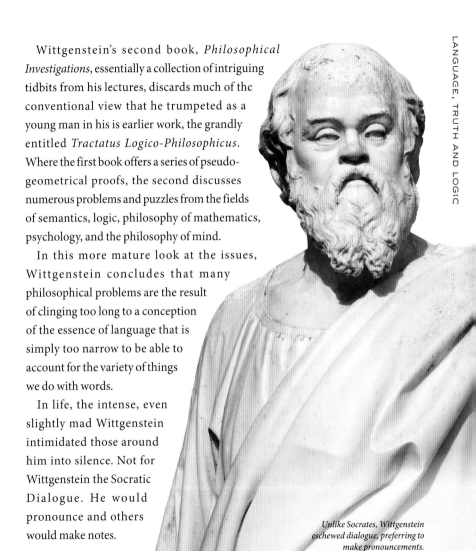

Wittgenstein's second book, *Philosophical Investigations*, essentially a collection of intriguing tidbits from his lectures, discards much of the conventional view that he trumpeted as a young man in his is earlier work, the grandly entitled *Tractatus Logico-Philosophicus*. Where the first book offers a series of pseudo-geometrical proofs, the second discusses numerous problems and puzzles from the fields of semantics, logic, philosophy of mathematics, psychology, and the philosophy of mind.

In this more mature look at the issues, Wittgenstein concludes that many philosophical problems are the result of clinging too long to a conception of the essence of language that is simply too narrow to be able to account for the variety of things we do with words.

In life, the intense, even slightly mad Wittgenstein intimidated those around him into silence. Not for Wittgenstein the Socratic Dialogue. He would pronounce and others would make notes.

Unlike Socrates, Wittgenstein eschewed dialogue, preferring to make pronouncements.

In one of his examples, Wittgenstein claims that looking for a flower and imagining one involves playing two different language games.

THE BARE FACTS

Wittgenstein starts with the startling claim that the world is a collection of 'facts'. That is, a chain of 'simples' or 'objects', Gegenstände, the ultimate building blocks of reality.

> 'Objects make up the substance of the world. That is why they cannot be composite. The substance of the world can only determine a form, and not any material properties… in a manner of speaking, objects are colourless… objects are what is unalterable and subsistent; their configuration is what is changing and unstable.'

The *Tractatus*, even in its later role as a doctoral thesis, does not offer any references or sources.

Yet we do not need to look very far to see a view not so very different, if not as strikingly posed as the numbered assertions of the *Tractatus*.

Russell and Leibniz both argue that knowledge is essentially a matter of analysing the 'building blocks' of reality and thereby guaranteeing the 'determinateness of sense' in language. This is the project of the *Tractatus*, too.

Russell's argument used metaphors from chemistry, talking of the task of creating 'molecular propositions' out of 'logical atoms', while Leibniz elegantly described possible complex arrangements of his logical monads.

Wittgenstein's *Tractatus* explains that language paints pictures of facts, and that, 'the propositions show the logical form of reality'. Russell himself, warning against grand 'system building' of the Leibnizian style, emphasised instead the need to identify the 'logical structure' of language, and the confusing ways in which it could differ from the 'grammatical' one.

This is essentially the project of the 'later Wittgenstein'. But the 'Young Impetuous Wittgenstein' declares in the Tractatus that it should, in principle at least, be possible to construct a new logically rigorous language.

Orbital model of an Atom.

Weininger wrote that each human is made of two parts, male and female, but the male part is best.

Of course, this new language will not deal with a lot of topics for (in the *Tractatus'* most quotable line), 'wherefore one cannot speak, thereof one must be silent'. Or as Otto Weininger more poetically puts it:

'Kant's solitary man laughs not, nor dances, shouts not, nor rejoices. For him, no need to make a noise, so deeply does the world expanse its silence keep'.

WITTGENSTEIN'S ONLY ACKNOWLEDGED INFLUENCE

Otto Weininger was, like Wittgenstein, Austrian. Like Wittgenstein, too, he published a book at a precociously early age. In his case, it was called *Geschlecht und Charakter* (*Sex and Character*). After his suicide at the age of 23, the book became very popular, going through 29 printings and multiple translations, including an English language version, which Wittgenstein passed around at Cambridge.

If his bemused colleagues had read it, they would have seen that Weininger's argument was that the highest form of human was a coolly logical male superhero, and that being homosexual, emotional or Jewish (such traits being 'feminine' in some sense) were all defects.

Each human has two parts, male and female, Weininger acknowledged, but it is best to be as male as possible. To be all female is to be reduced to the level of an animal – a view that Aristotle and others also had.

'Man is first entirely himself when he is entirely logical,' he wrote . The book was also aided by celebrity endorsements including the comment of one Adolf Hitler that Weininger was the 'only good Jew' he had ever heard of.

Adolf Hitler subscribed to many of Weininger's views.

LANGUAGE GAMES

Having explained why philosophy cannot answer life's most important questions, Wittgenstein put his money where his mouth was, and attempted, after publishing his theory, to exit philosophy.

But after some years he was back, taking up a fellowship and later a chair at Cambridge. Although he never committed himself again to print, many of his notes, comments and lectures, were collected and published.

The Wittgenstein revealed in these sees language as a series of interlinked 'language-games', in which words and sentences function in so many different and subtle ways: as 'deeds', as 'symbols', as 'commands'. Words, he says, (borrowing, as ever, in this case from Ferdinand de Saussure) are like pieces in a game of chess, taking on their meaning only in the context of the game.

Wittgenstein compared using words to a game of chess.

Wittgenstein, however, was in many ways only catching up with the linguist and semiotician, Ferdinand de Saussure (1857–1913), who had argued in the century before that it is the structure of language, rather than the rules of logic, that explains how we think and speak.

It was during the 19th century that linguistics became an academic discipline in its own right, and this was due in large part to the theorising of Saussure. The Swiss philosopher's central theme is that language is a system of signs which are in themselves arbitrary.

The proper subject matter for the study of a language is not individuals, but communities of language users, says Saussure.

By distinguishing thus between the language and the faculty of language, Saussurre says that it becomes clear that language is a 'product' or more precisely, a 'social product'.

The Swiss linguist Ferdinand de Saussure.

Saussure believed there were similarities between language and music.

Spoken language is the operation of the vocal apparatus, which is a mere action. But the underlying language is there in the brains of a set of individuals (belonging to the same language community), and there even when they are asleep. Saussure suggests that in each of these heads is the whole product that we call the language:

> 'The language, in turn, is quite
> independent of the individual;
> it cannot be a creation of the
> individual, it is essentially social;
> it presupposes the collectivity.'

Third Course of Lectures on General Linguistics (1910–1911)

Structuralism is very obscure and full of jargon, but the core idea is simple. This is that it is the structure of language, rather than the rules of logic, that explain how we think and how we speak.

Saussure resurrects an older distinction, between the structure of language, called 'langue', and manifestations of langue, which are called 'parole'. Saussure compares the two with an analogy: langue is the score for a piece of music, and parole is one particular performance of it.

Saussure thought that a particular sign's role in langue is determined by its relationships to the other signs in the system – its place in the structure. For example, the correct use of the vowel 'a' in English can vary subtly between the two words 'very and 'vary', or indeed between 'merry' and 'Mary' However, this example raises the issue of different ways of pronouncing words within a language community. Some people will pronounce 'Merry Christmas' as 'Mary Christmas',

for example, without it causing any confusion to the listener.

Another issue concerns Ferdinand de Saussure's statement that 'Groups of signs… themselves are signs.' This begs the question of how do you know of any sign that is not in fact composed of smaller, subsidiary ones?

It begins to look like every word and phrase has a multitude of potential uses and meanings, fixed only imprecisely in a web of shared cultural understandings and conventions.

Perhaps because of such untidy problems, structuralists tend to prefer to study the supposedly 'deep structures of grammar rather than the superficial forms of language use. Similarly, when structuralism migrated to other social sciences it tended to look for general rules. In English literature departments, the emphasis became on narrative rather than on boring old content or linguistic style.

It was Vygotsky's contention that speaking involved 'restructuring' thought.

Vygotsky also believed children perceive the world through language.

Saussure accepted that the signs for meaning are, of course, arbitrary. The important thing is to look beneath this layer at the rules – the hidden signifying system. The Russian psychologist, Lev Vygotsky (1896-1934) offers that:

> 'The structure of speech is not simply the mirror image of the structure of thought. It cannot, therefore, be placed on thought like clothes off a rack. Speech does not merely serve as the expression of developed thought. Thought is restructured as it is transformed into speech. It is not expressed but completed in the word.

> *Therefore, precisely because of the contrasting directions of movement, the development of the internal and external aspects of speech form a true identity.'*

Vygotsky says that children perceive the world though language as well as through their five senses. This is also the theme of Benjamin Lee Whorf.

Whorf likened the Ancient Greeks to the American Indians, which may seem odd, but in terms of philosophy of language, it makes sense, as the work of this unconventional and extra-academic thinker in the first half of the 20th century illustrates.

Whorf studied the languages of Native Americans.

A DIFFERENT VIEW

Whorf came from somewhere very different from the rest of the linguistic scholars and was happy to upset the conventions for the study of language.

As an insurance investigator, Whorf was originally interested in the mistakes people make with concepts and words, but he later made a detailed study of American Indian languages, discovering, he thought, radical differences in their structures.

This led him to suppose that, instead of trying to make language follow logical rules, we should realise that logic only seeks to institutionalise the accidents of Western grammar, and in as much as it succeeds in doing so, only creates a misleading view of the world. Neither language nor yet concepts were universal at all.

For example, according to Whorf, the passage of time is a creation of linguistic structures. Past, present and future are not 'out there' but 'in here', in our heads, or to be precise, in our grammars.

Whorf had been brought up on the mysteries of ciphers and puzzles, and as a young man read widely on botany, astrology, Mexican history, Mayan archaeology and photography.

He came to anthropology via an unusual mix of physics, Jungian synchronicity, systems theory and Gestalt psychology, but, above all, through linguistics – all of which interests he had been able to pursue only in his spare time.

Whorf decided that other language traditions were nearer to understanding reality because they represented their universe as having instead just two aspects – being and becoming.

Yet even a 'one dimensional', momentary universe is not so hard to accept from our individual perspectives, stuck as we are, in that 'infinitely brief moment of the present, as the river of time gushes out of nothingness, producing the bottomless lake of the past, whilst the future does not exist at all…

Whorf developed a keen interest in Mexican history and Mayan archaeology.

Of course, to all of us trapped within our 'house of language' this seems a very strange thing to claim. But Western languages, can be thought of as being static, orientated towards patterns, whereas languages like Hopi are actively concerned with processes.

The most significant difference between these two orientations is over that issue of identity that Aristotle's laws were supposed to settle.

A ceramic pot of the Hopi people whose language Whorf studied in depth.

'Empty' gasoline drums encouraged carelessness.

LINGUISTIC INSIGHTS IN EVERYDAY EVENTS

Whorf's day-job was as Investigator and Engineer for the Hartford Fire Insurance Company.

Within his work he came across many examples of what he would later see as language influencing thought patterns, and when his linguistic theory appeared in several influential articles it was set around the topic of fire prevention.

People, he observed in the first of these articles, tended to be careless around 'empty drums' of gasoline; drums, that is, 'empty' of petrol but equally 'full' of vapours more explosive than the liquid. He noticed how people were complacent towards industrial 'waste water' and 'spun limestone', both, again flammable and dangerous, perhaps because of the impressions of stability that the words 'water' and 'stone' convey.

In the 1920s, still working full time, he entered into correspondence with the leading US scholars of the day and from 1931 he studied Linguistics (part-time) under Edward Sapir, one of the key figures in the new discipline of socio-linguistics.

It was at this time that he made his in-depth study of the language structures of the Hopi Indians and a stream of detailed, almost poetic papers established his reputation.

THE CENTRAL IDEA OF LINGUISTIC RELATIVITY

'We dissect nature along lines laid down by our native languages. The categories and types that we isolate from the world of phenomena we do not find there because they stare every observer in the face; on the contrary, the world is presented in a kaleidoscopic flux of impressions which has to be organised by our minds – and this means largely by the linguistic systems in our minds. We cut nature up, organise it into concepts, and ascribe significances as we do, largely because we are parties to an agreement that holds throughout our speech community and is codified in the patterns of our language.'

The agreement is, of course, 'an implicit and unstated one', Whorf continues, but 'its terms are absolutely obligatory; we cannot talk at all except by subscribing to the organisation and classification of data which the agreement decrees.'

Perhaps the problem is really that his arguments appear to elevate the thinking of the American Indian over the thinking of the American academic, a scandalous supposition made much worse by being couched in scientific language.

As the American psychology professor, John Lucy puts it: 'For some [linguistic relativity], represents a threat to the very possibility of reasoned inquiry.' Whorf, he explains, threatens the legitimacy of the activities of conventional researchers looking for 'objective facts' and 'reality'.

Whorf's groundbreaking work on the language patterns of the Indians of North America is not taken very seriously by mainstream academics. Noam Chomsky describes his work as 'entirely premature', not based on enough evidence, and 'lacking in precision'.

Representing mainstream academic philosophy, Robert Kirk says that Whorf offers little more than truisms – an apparently contradictory objection.

Whorf studied how language could affect the way people interpreted the world.

RULES OF LANGUAGE

Even were Whorf to be shown to be absolutely right about the nature of language, 'his correct guess would have been based on no evidence of substance and no defensible formal analysis of English structure,' Chomsky complains.

The American philosopher and linguist, Noam Chomsky believes that the rules of grammar are hard-wired into our brains.

But then, Chomsky had his own contribution to linguistics to defend.

In the 20th century, Chomsky had argued that the rules of a language are hard-wired into all of us – that grammar is a kind of 'deep structure' embedded physically in the brain. This is how young infants can learn language without apparently having sufficient exposure to examples to 'generate' it from nothing, in the manner supposed by simple notions of human learning. Chomsky is given a lot of credit for this insight, which fits very well supposedly modern theories of 'how the brain works'.

In fact, Chomsky's deep structure looks very like Plato's idea of the knowledge of the heavenly forms being present in all minds, even

Like Plato, Chomsky believes that certain crucial knowledge is innate, not learned.

Meno's slave boy, and only need to be gently remembered.

Modern linguists hate this sort of approach and prefer to look to biochemistry for explanations of how languages work.

Populists like Stephen Pinker have called it 'unintentionally comic'. Pinker, a contemporary philosopher who normally describes himself more imposingly as a 'cognitive scientist' says in his own book, called *The Language Instinct,* that the idea that thought is the same thing as language 'is an example of what can be called a conventional absurdity.'

Pinker takes up Whorf's example of the gasoline containers, for instance.

Whorf says the use of the word 'empty' on a sign by the metal gasoline drums led workers to think of the drums as 'empty', void, 'full of nothing', when in reality the drums were full of inflammable residues.

In order to reassert order in the linguistic world, Pinker instead insists the workers' error is because the gas drums look empty – so the confusion is empirical, not linguistic, after all.

Since steel gasoline drums tend not to be see-through, this argument weakens somewhat, but Whorf's point is rather different anyway. He is pointing out that when the workers mentally categorised the drums as 'empty', they adopted a linguistic model of 'empty' containers that led them to perceive no hazard.

Pinker instead sketches out the latest thinking on how the mind works saying:

Pinker contends that the eye sees , and responds to, visual stimuli automatically regardless of the influence of language.

'... the cells of the eye are wired to neurones in a way that makes neurones respond [to certain colours]. No matter how influential language might be, it would seem preposterous to a physiologist that it could reach down into the retina and rewire the ganglion cells.'

Pinker's explanation allows no room for things like consciousness, which is an entity which Cognitive Scientists do not believe in. For them, the brain is just a biological computer.

'In the brain, there might be three groups of neurones, one used to represent the individual that the proposition is about (Socrates, Rod Stewart, and so on [Pinker's witticism]), one to represent the logical relationship in the proposition (is a, is not, is like, and so on), and one to represent the class or type that the individual is being characterised as (men, dogs chickens, and so on).

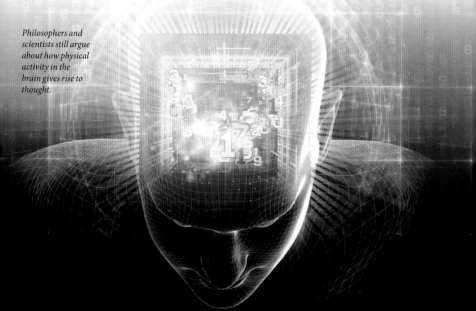

Philosophers and scientists still argue about how physical activity in the brain gives rise to thought.

Each concept corresponds to the firing of a particular neurone. The processor might be a network of other neurones feeding into these groups, connected together. This says Pinker, is the 'computational' theory of mind.

Ideas come and go. In fact, Whorf's one of linguistic relativity was by no means new. The 19th century founder of linguistics, Baron Wilhelm von Humboldt had argued that thought would be completely impossible without language, and, equally, that language completely determined thought – the view that Whorf, incorrectly, is often claimed to have argued, too.

In actual fact, Whorf's aim was to update the older philosophical theory with some of the new physics of the early 20th century. Indeed, at this time, Von Humboldt's theory was taking on renewed life with the new theory of 'relativity' ruling everything in physics – and Einstein himself even cited Von Humboldt in a radio programme.

In one of his essays, later collected together into the book, *Language, Thought, and Reality*, (1956), Whorf says:

> *'Just as it is possible to have any number of geometries other than the Euclidean which give an equally perfect account of space configurations, so it is possible to have descriptions of the universe, all equally valid, that do not contain our familiar contrasts of time and space. The relativity viewpoint of modern physics is one such view, conceived in mathematical terms, and the Hopi weltanschauung is another and quite different one, non-mathematical and linguistic....'*

And Whorf goes on to challenge the Newtonian worldview – permanent and unchanging like Plato's Forms. It is this that so alarmed the philosophers, rather than anything merely linguistic.

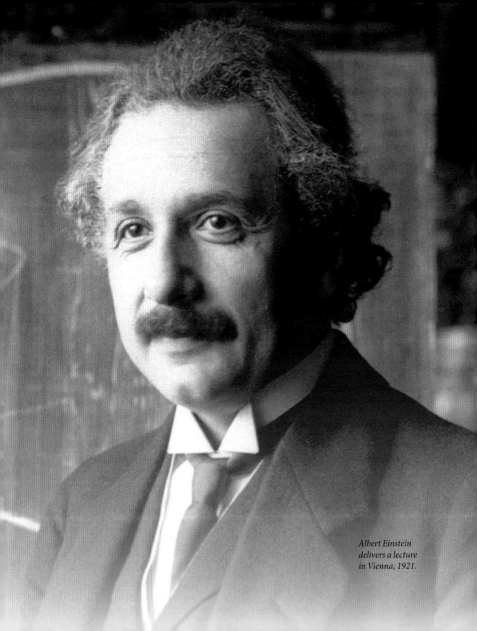

Albert Einstein delivers a lecture in Vienna, 1921.

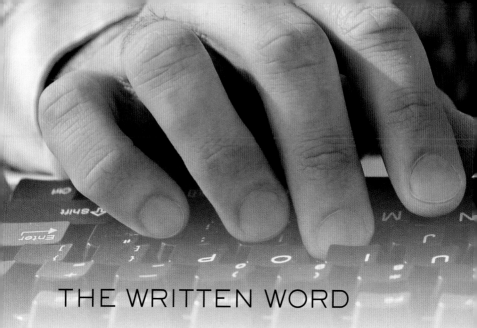

THE WRITTEN WORD

In the late 20th century, the French philosopher Jacques Derrida returned to Ferdinand de Saussure's description of the workings of language, and attempted to 'deconstruct it'.

In the process, he claimed to prove that in seeking to provide a list of distinctions between writing and speech, the Father of Structuralism has inadvertently produced a list of characteristics of thinking – it is arbitrary in form, material and relative – that apply as much to speech as to writing!

The difference between speech and writing is thus revealed as nothing more than a philosophical illusion.

Following this successful deconstruction of the speech/writing distinction, came the end of the soul-body one (vide Descartes); the collapsing of the difference between things knowable by the mind and

things knowable by sense perception; the rejection of distinctions between literal and metaphorical, between natural and cultural creations, between masculine and feminine... and yet more:

'All dualisms, all theories of the immortality of the soul or of the spirit, as well as all monisms, spiritualist or materialist, dialectical or vulgar, are the unique theme of metaphysics whose entire history was compelled to strive towards the reduction of the trace.

'The subordination of the trace to the full presence summed up in the logos, the humbling of writing beneath a speech dreaming as pleniture, such are the gestures required by an onto-theology determining the archaeological and eschatological meaning of being as presence, as parousia, as life without différance: another name for death, historical metonymy where God's name holds death in check.'

Of Grammatology

355

Derrida argues that there can be no 'meaning' as there is nothing fixed within the great web of language, or indeed life and perception. Everything is a mirage, or what's worse, a kind of 'fine powder' residue left behind by boiling off our politico-sexual assumptions.

Loaded terms like 'is' that discriminate against 'is not', or 'me' that is set against 'you'. We must destroy the web of words!

'This interweaving, this textile, is the text produced only in the transformation of another text. Nothing neither among the elements nor within the system, is anywhere ever simply present or absent. There are everywhere, differences and traces of traces.'

Semiology and Grammatology

'The play of differences supposes in effect, syntheses and referrals which forbid, at any moment, or in any sense, that a simple element be present in and of itself, referring only to itself. Whether in the order of spoken or written discourse, no element can function as a sign without referring to another element which itself is not simply present...

But it is very hard to follow what Derrida is saying. What was that transcendental-thingummy again? After all, Derrida himself liked to offer contradictions and to refuse definitions when asked to explain things.

At various times, he has insisted that deconstruction itself is not a method, nor an act performed, as it were, on a text by a subject. Indeed, he once declared in his 'Letter to a Japanese Friend', that it is never possible to say either that 'deconstruction is such and such' or 'deconstruction is not such and such', for the construction (yes) of the sentence would be such that is false already.

It is a grand position to be sure, to coin a phrase and then to deny others the ability to make any pronouncements whatsoever on the new term. Yet Derrida acknowledges a certain influence from the German philosopher, Heidegger, who, anxious to expose the bankruptcy of Western civilisation and 'humanism' in general, had an earlier philosophical project which he had called 'Dekonstruktion'.

Heidegger borrowed many of the aims of his project – 'transcendental phenomenology' – from another philosopher (Edmund Husserl) and the term itself comes from a Nazi psychiatry journal edited by a cousin of Hermann Göring.

Harvard Universiy, Cambridge, Massachusetts USA, where Derrida studied from 1956–57.

Bagels, the breakfast of philosophers.

And that's not even to mention Heidegger's long and enthusiastic participation in the Nazi party. Anyway, what is said to be noteworthy about Heidegger's project is that it both highlights and challenges the role of time in our structuring of the world, both in our minds and in our writing of texts.

From Heidegger, along with destruktion , Derrida also takes the notion of 'presence'. Heidegger's footprints are there too in the concept of 'Being', and the difference between beings and Being, which Heidegger calls the 'ontico-ontological difference'.

Derrida refers obliquely back to this at one point in his book called (not entirely coincidentally) *Writing and Difference* when he defines *différance* as 'the pre-opening of the ontico-ontological difference'.

The fact is, looking at Derrida's writings, very little of it is original, and maybe it's not worth struggling through it all. If that seems weak-spirited, recall the message of a cinematic biography of the great philosopher – *Derrida the Movie* – which was released in 2002. This depicted Derrida as a joker, as 'one of us'. His Jewish origins, for example, are shown by his having bagels for breakfast; his self-doubt by his worrying about the colour co-ordination of his clothes.

At one point, as the camera follows him into his library, packed with thousands of books, the philosopher is asked: 'Have you read all the books in here?'

'Why no,' Derrida replies, 'only four of them. But I read these very, very carefully.'

Perhaps we might say the same thing. Have we read all of Derrida? Why no, only a few paragraphs. But we have now read these, very, very carefully.

CHAPTER 10

BEYOND SCIENCE: PHILOSOPHERS STILL SEARCHING FOR WISDOM

'Only science can tell us about the world: it is the final arbiter of the truth.'

W. V. O. Quine

*For many, it is science, not philosophy that will
ultimately reveal the essential truths about the world.*

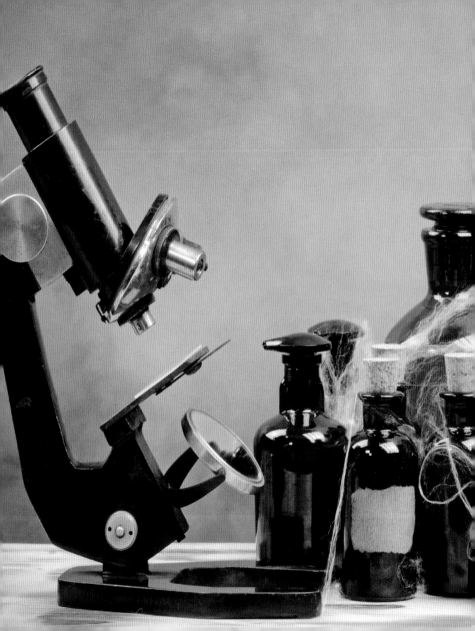

TRUTH AT LAST?

Science, not philosophy is 'the final arbiter of the truth' – that's the view of the contemporary American philosophy professor, W. V. O. Quine, who never, we can be sure, actually dabbled in any science himself.

Bust of the British philosopher, Bertrand Russell in Red Lion Square, London.

But he didn't need to because his remark correctly captures the spirit of the times. In an article titled 'Is There a God?' commissioned, but never published, by *Illustrated* magazine in 1952, Bertrand Russell gave a colourful example for a very similar view:

'If I were to suggest that between the Earth and Mars there is a china teapot revolving about the sun in an elliptical orbit, nobody would be able to disprove my assertion provided I were careful to add that the teapot is too small to be revealed even by our most powerful telescopes.

'But if I were to go on to say that, since my assertion cannot be disproved, it is intolerable presumption on the part of human reason to doubt it, I should rightly be thought to be talking nonsense.

'If, however, the existence of such a teapot were affirmed in ancient books, taught as the sacred truth every Sunday, and instilled into the *minds of children at school, hesitation to believe in its existence would become a mark of eccentricity and entitle the doubter to the attentions of the psychiatrist in an enlightened age or of the Inquisitor in an earlier time.'*

Russell and Quine reflect a conservative view of how knowledge works, with a comfortable assumption of steady progress. It is the view really summed up in the writings of Auguste Comte (1798–1857) – or Isidore Auguste Marie François Xavier Comte if you really want to know his rather grand, full name.

Mercury   Venus   Earth   Mars   Jupiter   Saturn   Uranus   Neptune

A dramatic illustration of the 'Cosmic Teapot' theory.

Comte believed that the development of human thought followed certain set stages much like manufacturing a car.

Sometimes dubbed the 'father' of positivism', Comte offers what he imagines is a kind of updated religion for humanity, and a blueprint for a new social order in the *Cours de Philosophie Positive (Course on Positive Philosophy)*, 1892.

Here, Comte argues the history of human thought is a steady progress through three stages, which are essentially psychological, but he also sees it as reflecting human history.

First was the theological stage, during which people sought to discover the 'essential nature of things' and the ultimate cause of existence, interpreted as gods or God. Philosophers, Comte wrote then, were stuck at this stage, perpetually but fruitlessly pursuing these sorts of existential questions!

The good news, Comte thought, was that, in an industrial society, many other people moved on to the next stage, which he calls the metaphysical one.

This involves abstract theory, although there is still a yearning for imagined underlying ethical values.

The final stage comes when people confine themselves to logical deduction from observed phenomena. This is the so-called scientific (or positive) stage.

> 'Now each of us is aware, if he looks back on his own history, that he was a theologian in his childhood, a metaphysician in his youth and a natural philosopher in his manhood.'

Don't be confused, here a 'natural philosopher' is not someone who naturally is good at philosophy but someone who studies nature – a scientist.

Emile Durkheim (1858–1917), born the year after Comte's death, took a different approach. He agrees that there is a kind of evolution to human society, which he interprets as a trend towards increased individualism at the expense of collective life.

The explanation and the driving force is in economics – the division of

The final stage in Comte's theory sees people's thoughts deriving only from direct scientific observation.

labour requires a division of society and a diversity of beliefs and values. Nonetheless, Durkheim insists that for society to exist, there has to be an overarching shared vision which is created out of shared ethical values.

COLLECTIVE LIFE

Durkheim returns to Comte's point that 'cooperation, far from having produced society, necessarily supposes, as preamble, its spontaneous existence.'

He sees important similarities between human society and say, an animal colony, such as a beehive, 'whose members embody a continuity of tissue from one individual'. In these colonies, the aggregate of individuals who are in continuous contact form a society.

Durkheim says that practical considerations ultimately bring people together into societies: factors such as living in the same land, sharing the same ancestors and gods, having the same traditions.

He warns that Rousseau, Hobbes, and even the utilitarians, all disregard the important social truth, that society predates the individual.

Durkheim believed there were many similarities between human societies and bee colonies.

According to Weber, the Industrial Revolution was largely the result of the beliefs and ethics of Protestants.

Weber, like Durkheim, made use of statistical observations to investigate the nature of human society. Like Durkheim, too, he claimed to have discovered important differences between Protestants and Catholics, with implications for social reality.

'Collective life is not born from individual life, but it is, on the contrary, the second which is born from the first... Cooperation is... the primary fact of moral and social life.'

Max Weber (1864–1920), as well as, to some extent, J. S. Mill, determined to carry on Comte's project and to further develop the science of society, even if the latter also accused Comte of having devised a 'despotism' of society over the individual.

Weber's particular insight is set out in his best known work, *The Protestant Ethic and the Spirit of Capitalism*. His view is that the Industrial Revolution in Europe was linked to the rejection of traditional Catholic religious practice in favour of a Protestant ideology which he interpreted as emphasizing the virtues of hard work.

A second strand to this new way of thinking was that material goods and wealth became virtuous in the sense that they were to looked upon as rewards, reflecting God's approval of one's efforts.

367

The German sociologist, philosopher and political economist, Max Weber.

The Protestant religion provided the new breed of capitalists, Weber thought, with an ideological double whammy: their wealth was virtuous, and they were under no obligations to raise the material standard of living of their workers.

Weber and Durkheim agree on the key principle that the social arrangement is prior to the economic, although Weber is not necessarily in favour of this. In *The Origin of Modern Capitalism*, he says that 'in the East it was essentially ritualistic considerations, including caste and clan organisations, which prevented the development of a deliberate economic policy' and that capitalism could only develop once a powerful political administration was created, as in the British parliamentary system with its powerful tier of professional bureaucrats.

Weber was employed as a bureaucrat himself – a hospital administrator during the First World War. Perhaps this gave him a more generous opinion of the value of such activities than that of other academics, sheltered from practical tasks in their ivory towers. Weber wants society run by bureaucrats, who use 'value-free' systems – 'value free', that is, apart from the underlying assumption that rationality is good.

And bureaucracies, Weber thinks, naturally promote a 'rationalist' way of life, just as rationality itself is inclined to prefer government according to rules, rather than mere authority. Weber was particularly impressed by the new highly organised German state under Bismarck – even if he was also concerned at the threats it posed to individual liberties.

For Weber, as for Durkheim, it was not enough to explain society and social activity in terms of causes and mechanisms – there must be a purpose. This, he says emphatically, is normally an economic one.

Other purposes and traditions are undesirable as they hinder economic progress. Similarly, when behaviour is affected by emotions and passions; which he calls 'affectual action', it is an obstacle to rational decision-making. Weber says that society should be ordered by a strong authority that needs to be respected, almost worshipped.

MAX WEBER
—
DIE PROTESTANTISCHE
ETHIK
UND DER GEIST
DES KAPITALISMUS

German edition of The Protestant Ethic and the Spirit of Capitalism.

Comte and Weber are long on logic and short on feeling. Durkheim, however, despite being usually remembered for statistical examinations of social trends, also writes in a very different way about the nature of society, exploring both myths and metaphors.

However, in this area, it is Claude Levi-Strauss, who offers the most intriguing examination of the nature of modern societies which he achieves, perhaps paradoxically, by comparing them to older, 'primitive' ones.

The Native American tradition for example, places a great emphasis on animism, which is the view that everything in the universe has a spiritual aspect, and not just things we normally imagine to be alive, from people to favoured animals.

The French anthropologist, Claude Lévi-Strauss.

Levi-Strauss identifies certain constants that all societies have and uses the simpler societies as a way of revealing them more dramatically. For example, he says that the whole notion of modern psychiatry, per Freud, is essentially an attempt to come to terms with the opposition created between 'nature' and 'society', between the individual and the environment they exist in.

Analogy and metaphor are central to the structures of thought, (Levi-Strauss proposes). Dreams and premonitions need to be accorded equal status to conventional senses as ways in which the mind interacts with reality.

This is a long way from the views of Quine and Russell at the start of this chapter, or indeed of John Horgan, sometime editor of the *Scientific American* magazine, who once opined in a talk entitled 'Why I Think Science Is Ending':

'I believe that this map of reality that scientists have constructed, and this narrative of creation, from the big bang through the present, is essentially true. It will thus be as viable 100 or even 1,000 years from now as it is today.

'I also believe that, given how far science has already come, and given the limits constraining further research, science will be hard-pressed to make any truly profound additions to the knowledge it has already generated. Further research may yield no more great revelations or revolutions but only incremental returns.'

The American science journalist John Horgan, author of The End of Science.

Throughout history, there has been both cooperation and competition between science and faith.

CLASH OF IDEAS

The gulf between science and philosophy is rather as Paul Feyerabend (of whose background and ideas more later) describes in another talk this time entitled 'How To Defend Society Against Science'.

Which perspective is correct? Is science really the systematic piecing together of facts about the universe, a process now almost complete, or an unending assembling and disassembling of competing ideas and theories – politics by another name?

All scientific theories, let alone 'facts' are open to challenge, on this or other ground, from this or that perspective. Stop a moment to consider what we mean by scientific facts anyway. The most conservative scientist will accept that the body of knowledge is not so much cast in stone but organically developing. It seems, as far as textbooks go, that in 30 years, every component fact will have changed: the age of the universe, how it was created, how life began, how DNA works, even how to cook spaghetti...

Science is rather about choosing theories that best suit our purposes. Paul Feyerabend again:

'Wherever we look we see that great scientific advances are due to outside interference which is made to prevail in the face of the most basic and most 'rational' methodological rules. The lesson is plain: there does not exist a single argument that could be used to support the exceptional role which science today plays in society.'

How To Defend Society
Against Science

One of the great mysteries of modern times, the structure of DNA, was discovered in 1953.

The problem is not that politicians are making bad choices from the theories that are presented. Rather, it is the idea that experts know almost everything.

That idea is challenged by the 'rationalists', meaning thinkers such as Descartes, Leibniz and, above all, Kant, and 'classical empiricism', as revived and refined by the logical positivists of the so-called 'Vienna Circle' in the 1930s. Such people insisted that actual, tangible experiments had to settle the big scientific questions, and where they could not, the questions were nonsensical.

Against all these, the is an alternative perspective which is that there are no 'theory-free', infallible observations as empiricists ask us to assume, but rather, all observation is theory-laden, and involves seeing the world through the distorting glass (and filter) of a pre-existing conceptual scheme.

Or, to put it another way, the problem is that (as Hume pointed out) no number of positive confirmations at the level of experimental testing can ever really confirm a scientific theory.

Yet this has not dented the scientific edifice one little bit. Instead, scientists take up the methodological lifebelt that was thrown out by Karl Popper (1902–1994), who is often counted as one of the great philosophers of science. Popper agrees that science must be fated to perceive the world only indirectly, thorough the ever distorting glass of existing theory.

The central thrust of his argument, however, is entirely Socratic, that knowledge-seeking becomes a process of rooting out a counter-example to demolish old theories with the intention of producing new, better ones in their place.

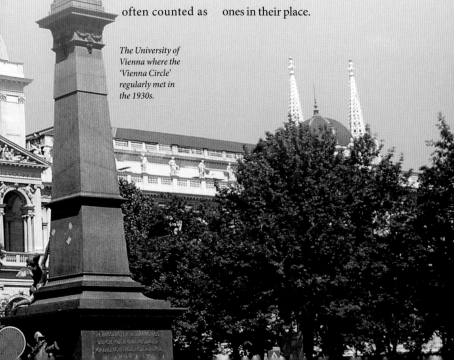

The University of Vienna where the 'Vienna Circle' regularly met in the 1930s.

Popper says that: 'tests can be interpreted as attempts to weed out false theories – to find the weak points of a theory in order to reject it if it is falsified by the test.

'This view is sometimes considered paradoxical; our aim, it is said, is to establish theories, not to eliminate false ones. But just because it is our aim to establish theories as well as we can, we must test them as severely as we can; that is, we must try to find fault with them.

'Only if we cannot falsify them despite our best efforts can we say they have stood up to severer tests. This is why the discovery of instances in which a theory means very little if we have not tried, and failed, to discover refutations. For if we are uncritical, we shall always find what we want: we shall look for, and find confirmations, and we shall look away from and not see, whatever might be dangerous to our pet theories.'

Representing the conventional view of scientists patiently conducting experiments to 'test' out their theories in reality, Popper maintains that, when the results do not accord with those anticipated, they are supposed to accept that their theory is 'disproven, or 'falsified' to use the term popularised by Popper in his book, *The Poverty of Historicism* (1957).

However, the modification of the Ptolemaic System, that is the Ancient Greek theories of how the heavenly bodies might be on crystal spheres, is itself a 'paradigm' demonstration of how 'falsification' does not seem to take place, let alone decide the survival or otherwise of a theory.

Instead, the Ancients simply increased the number of spheres each time observations showed a problem for the theory. It is here that the really rather psychological and obscure notion of the 'paradigm shift' comes in.

Sir Karl Raimund Popper was an Austrian-British philosopher and professor.

Kuhn saw science as a 'building erected on piles'.

DEMOLISHING SCIENCE

In a landmark, 1962 book, called The Structure of Scientific Revolutions, *Thomas Kuhn offers a way to square falsification with the evidence that scientists, in reality, ignore facts that go against them.*

He explains that the popularly imagined lofty and impregnable fortress of scientific consensus is really just a façade. Demolishing the edifice does not even require a loud bang.

Instead, working and otherwise 'more-than-my-jobs-worth' scientists may collectively abandon the consensus theory for something that seems to suit them better, or for any number of reasons, none of them particularly scientific let alone dramatic.

In *The Logic of Scientific Discovery*, Karl Popper offers this analogy for the state of 'normal science':

> 'Science does not rest upon solid bedrock. The bold structure of its

theories rises, as it were, above a swamp. It is like a building erected on piles... if we stop driving the piles deeper, it is not because we have reached firm ground. We simply stop when we are satisfied that the piles are firm enough to carry the structure, at least for the time being.'

It is a nice analogy, even if the philosophical perception of science remains firmly rooted in a Platonic universe of eternal and unchanging truths. One of the surprising lessons of the history of science is that analogies like this get us further than either rigid 'rules' or grand theories. In fact, in area after area of science, breakthroughs take place at the level of creative analogy, rather than in the sifting and analysis of precise data.

Take that most celebrated equation: $E=mc^2$, or energy = mass times the velocity of light squared. This is directly and significantly analogous to a much more mundane relationship in mechanics: the one that says that kinetic energy = mass times velocity squared (albeit divided by two).

The American academic, Douglas Hofstadter.

The point has been made by Douglas Hofstadter recently. Hofstadter is an American 'cognitive scientist', who noted in a popular book called *Gödel, Escher, Bach: An Eternal Golden Braid* (1979) that 'fuzzy' thinking in many areas, including what we think of as hard science, is essential.

Hofstadter is reacting to the orthodoxy described by Thomas Kuhn with his picture of a 'normal science' predicated on the assumption that 'the scientific community knows what the world is like'– and that, within it, new ideas, new paradigms or theories, have to be suppressed because they are 'necessarily subversive' of basic commitments. In Kuhn's view, within normal science:

'Novelty emerges only with difficulty, manifested by resistance.'

He explains that this is because scientists function without a set of beliefs. If a paradigm is essential to scientific inquiry:

'... no natural history can be interpreted in the absence of at least some implicit body of intertwined theoretical and methodological belief that permits selection, evaluation, and criticism.'

We should recall the argument of Paul Feyerabend in more detail. Feyerabend was the Austrian-born, but US based, philosopher of science of the second half of 20th century, who was renowned for his anarchistic view of science and his rejection of the existence of universal methodological rules. He worked for most of his career as a professor of philosophy – not a scientist – at the University of California, although he also lived in Britain, Italy and Switzerland.

The UC Berkeley campus where Paul Feyerabend was a professor of philosophy.

Feyerabend's best-known works are polemics against what he sees as simple-minded science – books such as *Against Method* (1975), *Science in a Free Society* (1978) and *Farewell to Reason* (1987).

Feyerabend compared his campaign against the various theories of 'empty sophistication' to fighting the Hydra of Greek myth.

'Methodology has by now become so crowded with empty sophistication that it is extremely difficult to perceive the simple errors at the basis.

It is like fighting the hydra – cut off one ugly head, and eight formalizations take its place. In this situation the only answer is superficiality: when sophistication loses content then the only way of keeping in touch with reality is to be crude and superficial. This is what I intend to be.'

Feyerabend insists that the progress of science, of good science, depends on novel ideas and on intellectual freedom, and reminds us that science has very often been advanced by outsiders.

To be fair, Thomas Kuhn (and most of the others) will also allow that 'evidence' alone does not decide theories. Kuhn notes that philosophers of science have repeatedly demonstrated that more than one theoretical construction can always be placed upon a given collection of data.

It's just that, even if problems and weaknesses with a theory begin to accumulate, he says, it is easier for the establishment, scientific, religious, political, to either 'modify' the original idea, or more often to suppress the conflicting information, than to abandon their established orthodoxies.

However, it is another Kuhn, but no relation, who raises the more specific question about the extent to which logical rules and the methods of rational argument, in fact, underlie the beliefs people hold and the judgements and decisions that they make.

Deanna Kuhn, a modern US professor of Psychology and Education, believes that 'thinking as argument' is implicit in all the beliefs people hold, in all the judgments they make, and finally in all the conclusions that people come to.

'Argumentation' arises every time a significant decision must be made. Hence, it is at the heart of what we should be interested in and concerned about in examining people's thinking.'

Some philosophers think that many scientific theories are based less on observable facts than pre-existing beliefs.

In other words, we should see thinking as a form of argument because our beliefs are chosen from among alternatives on the basis of the evidence for them.

However, her own research has led Kuhn increasingly to question the extent to which individuals actually do hold their beliefs on the basis of evidence rather than as a result of social pressures.

It is very ironic, she argues, that as a society we spend much of our time and effort determining what it is that we believe, we know and seem to care little about how it is we come to believe what we do.

She asks: Do people know why they believe what they do, in a way that they can justify to themselves and others? Do they even know what they believe, in the sense of being consciously aware of these beliefs as choices they have made among many different beliefs they might hold? Do they understand what sort of evidence would indicate that a belief should be modified or abandoned?

For Deanna Kuhn, the answer is rather alarming. It seems that many people do

As Deanna Kuhn notes, most people are sure the Earth orbits the Sun, but rather fewer can provide any good evidence to back up this belief.

not or cannot give adequate evidence for the beliefs they hold.

Worse! People are unwilling or unable to consider revising their beliefs when presented with evidence against them. She holds that reasoned argument requires, at the very least, this ability to distinguish between the theoretical framework and the physical evidence.

Raymond Tallis, the medical researcher and philosopher scientist, provides a plausible example of what

The positions of religion and science often seem to be directly opposed.

Deanna Kuhn may mean. Tallis is particularly appalled by what he calls the 'Darwinization of our understanding of humanity' as well as by 'neuromania' more generally, which he defines as the almost ubiquitous use of what is offered as the latest brain science to supposedly reveal how our minds work.

CAN SCIENTISTS REALLY SEE THOUGHTS IN OUR BRAINS?

Neuroscience is all about new technology. Yet even the latest MRI 'brain scanners' are not all they are made out to be. Forget all those colour pictures of people's brains as they are being shown images of 'loved ones', because even the best brain scanners can only measure brain activity by detecting the additional blood flow prompted by busy neurons.

According Raymond Talllis, neuronal activity lasts milliseconds, while detected changes in blood flow lag by 2–10 seconds, discrediting the precision of the method. Tallis also explains that many millions of neurons have to be activated in order to discern a change in blood flow, so this is hardly a way pinpointing particular thoughts.

Tallis accuses the experiments of being laughably crude. Subjects may be shown photographs of friends, and then of lovers, and the 'differences' in the brain scans taken to indicate the 'unconditional-love spot'.

More mundane tests with subjects being asked to tap their fingers shows the correlation between one test and the retests to be so poor that nothing can be deduced from the experiment.

How much less then can be deduced from the scans of our deepest emotions?

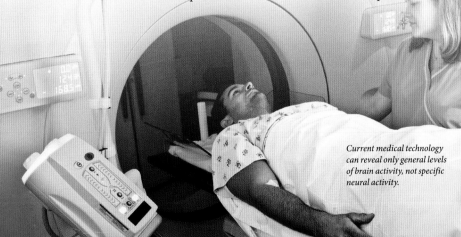

Current medical technology can reveal only general levels of brain activity, not specific neural activity.

The physiologist, Albrecht von Haller.

Neuromaniacs assume, because they have to, that there is some central controller of these neurons, a 'homunculus', or little man, inside the big man – something akin to the program that runs in a digital computer.

This conceit goes back a long way, and can be seen in Descartes or, as Tallis recommends, in the writings of the physiologist, Albrecht von Haller (1708–77) who wrote that there must be a 'principle part' of the brain in which sense data is processed and 'motions' are initiated.

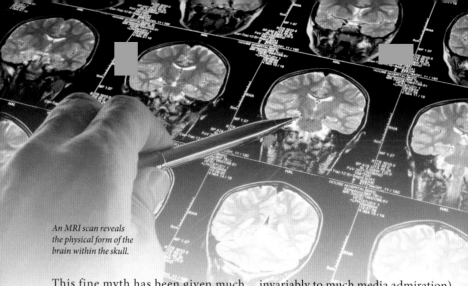

This fine myth has been given much apparent substance by new technology in recent years – notably by Functional Magnetic Resonance Imaging (fMRI).

It is fMRI, more than anything else, that has taken the analysis of brain function beyond the laboratory into the wider world of popular science, to the point where it is now almost impossible to pick up a newspaper without encountering an image of the brain, showing the location of love, or hatred, or wisdom.

Astonishing experiments by the neurophysiologist Benjamin Libet in the 1980s (repeated many times since, invariably to much media admiration) even seem to show that the human brain takes decisions to act before our conscious mind is aware of them.

Could it be then, newspaper pundits have rushed to ask, that our decisions are not really 'our' decisions? For some experts it seems a small step to conclude, but if it is a small step it is certainly one too far for Raymond Tallis. He protests:

> *'You would have to be pretty resistant to the overwhelming body of evidence to deny that the human brain is an evolved organ, fashioned by the processes of natural selection acting*

on spontaneous variation. It does not follow from this that the mind is, unless you believe that the mind is identical with brain activity.'

Aping Mankind

Tallis instead presses the contrary view that the human brain is an unimaginably complex nexus of neural circuits responding individually or sometimes collectively, or en masse, in highly specific ways to stimuli of various kinds. Indeed, to 'complexes of stimuli' – stimuli that create 'non-linear', unpredictable, even chaotic results. Add to which, 'What is now realised is that the way the neurons are wired together can be dramatically changed as a result of experience'.

In this way, the arguments of neuroscience must lead not only to the end of 'freewill' but also to the end of the individual 'self', the 'I'. Thus, nearly 400 years after Descartes made him king, the individual self is exposed as mere philosophical propaganda, that has no ultimate reality.

Tallis argues that the brain's 'unimaginably complex' neural circuits respond to stimuli in a variety of ways.

INDEX

ACKNOWLEDGMENTS

The publisher would would like to thank the following for their kind permission to reproduce their photographs:

The images on the following pages are Public Domain:

p2, p6, p9, p12, p14, p15, p22, p25, p27, p29, p31, p34, p35, p42, p43, p49, p56, p60, p61, p62, p64, p65, p67, p71, p73, p76, p77, p81 (right), p82, p83, p87 (top), p91, p94, p99, p107, p120, p145, p147, p160, p162, p189, p209, p211, p214, p215, p224, p231, p235, p250, p251, p260, p263, p268, p270, p276, p288, p299, p307, p311, p312, p317, p319, p323, p337, p344, p353, p369, p377, p387.

All other images are iStock.com unless stated otherwise:

p11 Matt Neale, p24 Bandan, p30 Erlend Bjørtvedt, p41 Tommy Wong, p53 Marie-Lan Nguyen, p55 Steven G. Johnson, p68 Keystone-France, p81 (left) Shutterstock.com, p84 Fb78, p87 (bottom) Sanchezn, p113 Sage Ross, p127 Andrew Dunn, p159 Marcelmulder68, p161 Rama, pp170–171 Vitold Muratov, p178 Andrew Dunn, p179 Fritzbruno, p182–183 NASA, p210 Jerrye & Roy Klotz, p213 David W Rogers, p225 Alex-hello, p230 Christian Bortes, p240 Kyselak, p249 Muesse, p258 www.marxists.org, p259 Diliff, p262 Shutterstock, p264 Shutterstock, p269 Viosan, p272 Simon Lee, p278 Jean-Pierre Dalbéra, p286 Husond, p292 Frank Behnsen, p315 Daderot, p348 Duncan Rawlinson, p363 Lonpicman, p370 UNESCO/Michel Ravassard, p371 Sage Ross, 374–375 Gryffindor, p380 Maurizio Codogno, p381 Charlie Nguyen.